The Miracle Worker

and Related Readings

McDougal Littell
A HOUGHTON MIFFLIN COMPANY
Evanston, Illinois • Boston • Dallas

Acknowledgments

Scribner: *The Miracle Worker* by William Gibson. Copyright © 1956, 1957 by William Gibson. Copyright © 1959, 1960 by Tamarack Productions, Ltd., and George S. Klein and Leo Garel as trustees under three separate deeds of trust. All rights reserved. This edition is reprinted by arrangement with Scribner, an imprint of Simon & Schuster Inc. Caution: *The Miracle Worker* is the sole property of the above named copyright Owners, and is fully protected by copyright. It may not be acted by professionals or amateurs without written permission and the payment of a royalty. All rights, including professional, amateur, stock, radio broadcasting, television, motion picture recitation, lecturing, public reading, and the rights of translation into foreign languages are reserved. All inquiries should be addressed to the Owners' agent, Flora Roberts, Inc., 157 W. 57th Street, Penthouse A, New York, NY 10019.

Doubleday: Excerpt from *Three Days to See* by Helen Keller. Copyright 1933 by Helen Keller. Used by permission of Doubleday, a division of Bantam Doubleday Dell Publishing Group, Inc.

The New York Times: "Darkness at Noon" by Harold Krents in *The New York Times*, May 26, 1976. Copyright © 1976 by The New York Times Co. Reprinted by permission of The New York Times.

Wallace Literary Agency, Inc.: "And Sarah Laughed" from *Rites of Passage* by Joanne Greenberg, published by Henry Holt & Co., 1972. Copyright © 1972 by Joanne Greenberg. Used by permission of the Wallace Literary Agency, Inc.

Continued on page 188

Cover illustration by Rafal Olbinski.
Author photo: AP/Wide World Photos.

2002 Impression

Printed in the United States of America.

ISBN 0-395-85803-8

8 9 10 11 12 13 14 15 – DCI –03 02

Contents

The Miracle Worker

William Gibson

A PLAY IN THREE ACTS

"*At another time she asked, 'What is a soul?' 'No one knows,' I replied; 'but we know it is not the body, and it is that part of us which thinks and loves and hopes.' . . . [and] is invisible. . . . 'But if I write what my soul thinks,' she said, 'then it will be visible, and the words will be its body.'*"

—ANNIE SULLIVAN, 1891

The playing space *is divided into two areas by a more or less diagonal line, which runs from downstage right to upstage left.*

The area *behind this diagonal is on platforms and represents the Keller house; inside we see, down right, a family room, and up center, elevated, a bedroom. On stage level near center, outside a porch, there is a water pump.*

The other area, *in front of the diagonal, is neutral ground; it accommodates various places as designated at various times—the yard before the Keller home, the Perkins Institution for the Blind, the garden house, and so forth.*

The convention of the staging *is one of cutting through time and place, and its essential qualities are fluidity and spatial counterpoint. To this end, the less set there is, the better; in a literal set, the fluidity will seem merely episodic. The stage therefore should be free, airy, unencumbered by walls. Apart from certain practical items—such as the pump, a window to climb out of, doors to be locked—locales should be only skeletal suggestions, and the movement from one to another should be accomplishable by little more than lights.*

CHARACTERS

A Doctor

Kate

Keller

Helen

Martha

Percy

Aunt Ev

James

Anagnos

Annie Sullivan

Viney

Blind Girls

A Servant

Offstage Voices

Time. The 1880's.

Place. In and around the Keller homestead in Tuscumbia, Alabama; also, briefly, the Perkins Institution for the Blind, in Boston.

ACT **ONE**

It is night over the Keller homestead.

Inside, three adults in the bedroom are grouped around a crib, in lamplight. They have been through a long vigil, and it shows in their tired bearing and disarranged clothing. One is a young gentlewoman with a sweet girlish face, Kate Keller; *the second is an elderly* Doctor, *stethoscope at neck, thermometer in fingers; the third is a hearty gentleman in his forties with chin whiskers,* Captain Arthur Keller.

Doctor. She'll live.

Kate. Thank God.

(*The* Doctor *leaves them together over the crib, packs his bag.*)

Doctor. You're a pair of lucky parents. I can tell you now, I thought she wouldn't.

Keller. Nonsense, the child's a Keller, she has the constitution of a goat. She'll outlive us all.

Doctor (*amiably*). Yes, especially if some of you Kellers don't get a night's sleep. I mean you, Mrs. Keller.

Keller. You hear, Katie?

Kate. I hear.

Keller (*indulgent*). I've brought up two of them, but this is my wife's first, she isn't battle-scarred yet.

Kate. Doctor, don't be merely considerate, will my girl be all right?

Doctor. Oh, by morning she'll be knocking down Captain Keller's fences again.

Kate. And isn't there anything we should do?

Keller (*jovial*). Put up stronger fencing, ha?

Doctor. Just let her get well, she knows how to do it better than we do.

(*He is packed, ready to leave.*)

Main thing is the fever's gone, these things come and go in infants, never know why. Call it acute congestion of the stomach and brain.

Keller. I'll see you to your buggy, Doctor.

Doctor. I've never seen a baby, more vitality, that's the truth.

(*He beams a good night at the baby and* Kate, *and* Keller *leads him downstairs with a lamp. They go down the porch steps, and across the yard, where the* Doctor *goes off left;* Keller *stands with the lamp aloft.* Kate *meanwhile is bent lovingly over the crib, which emits a bleat; her finger is playful with the baby's face.*)

Kate. Hush. Don't you cry now, you've been trouble enough. Call it acute congestion, indeed, I don't see what's so cute about a congestion, just because it's yours. We'll have your father run an editorial in his paper, the wonders of modern medicine, they don't know what they're curing even when they cure it. Men, men and their battle scars, we women will have to—

(*But she breaks off, puzzled, moves her finger before the baby's eyes.*)

Will have to—Helen?

(*Now she moves her hand, quickly.*)

Helen.

(*She snaps her fingers at the baby's eyes twice, and her hand falters; after a moment she calls out, loudly.*)

Captain. Captain, will you come—

(*But she stares at the baby, and her next call is directly at her ears.*)

Captain!

(*And now, still staring,* Kate *screams.* Keller *in the yard hears it, and runs with the lamp back to the house.* Kate *screams again, her look intent on the baby and terrible.* Keller *hurries in and up.*)

Keller. Katie? What's wrong?

Kate. Look.

(*She makes a pass with her hand in the crib, at the baby's eyes.*)

Keller. What, Katie? She's well, she needs only time to—

Kate. She can't see. Look at her eyes.

(*She takes the lamp from him, moves it before the child's face.*)

She can't *see!*

Keller (*hoarsely*). Helen.

Kate. Or hear. When I screamed she didn't blink. Not an eyelash—

Keller. Helen. Helen!

Kate. She can't *hear* you!

Keller. *Helen!*

(*His face has something like fury in it, crying the child's name; Kate almost fainting presses her knuckles to her mouth, to stop her own cry.*

The room dims out quickly.

Time, in the form of a slow tune of distant belfry chimes which approaches in a crescendo and then fades, passes; the light comes up again on a day five years later, on three kneeling children and an old dog outside around the pump.

The dog is a setter named Belle, *and she is sleeping. Two of the children are Negroes,* Martha and Percy. *The third child is* Helen, *six and a half years old, quite unkempt, in body a vivacious little person with a fine head, attractive, but noticeably blind, one eye larger and protruding; her gestures are abrupt, insistent, lacking in human restraint, and her face never smiles. She is flanked by the other two, in a litter of paper-doll cutouts, and while they speak* Helen's *hands thrust at their faces in turn, feeling baffledly at the movements of their lips.*)

Martha (*snipping*). First I'm gonna cut off this doctor's legs, one, two, now then—

Percy. Why you cuttin' off that doctor's legs?

Martha. I'm gonna give him a operation. Now I'm gonna cut off his arms, one, two. Now I'm gonna fix up—

(*She pushes* Helen's *hand away from her mouth.*)

You stop that.

Percy. Cut off his stomach, that's a good operation.

Martha. No, I'm gonna cut off his head first, he got a bad cold.

Percy. Ain't gonna be much of that doctor left to fix up, time you finish all them opera—

(*But* Helen *is poking her fingers inside his mouth, to feel his tongue; he bites at them, annoyed, and she jerks them away.* Helen *now fingers her own lips, moving them in imitation, but soundlessly.*)

Martha. What you do, bite her hand?

Percy. That's how I do, she keep pokin' her fingers in my mouth, I just bite 'em off.

Martha. What she tryin' do now?

Percy. She tryin' *talk.* She gonna get mad. Looka her tryin' talk.

(Helen *is scowling, the lips under her fingertips moving in ghostly silence, growing more and more frantic, until in a bizarre rage she bites at her own fingers. This sends* Percy *off into laughter, but alarms* Martha.)

Martha. Hey, you stop now.

(*She pulls* Helen's *hand down.*)

You just sit quiet and—

(*But at once* Helen *topples* Martha *on her back, knees pinning her shoulders down, and grabs the scissors.* Martha *screams.* Percy *darts to the bell string on the porch, yanks it, and the bell rings.*

Inside, the lights have been gradually coming up on the main room, where we see the family informally gathered, talking, but in pantomime. Kate *sits darning socks near a cradle, occasionally rocking it;* Captain Keller *in spectacles is working over newspaper pages at a table; a benign visitor in a hat,* Aunt Ev, *is sharing the sewing basket, putting the finishing touches on a big shapeless doll made out of towels; an indolent young man,* James Keller, *is at the window watching the children.*

With the ring of the bell, Kate *is instantly on her feet and out the door onto the porch, to take in the scene; now we see what these five years have done to her, the girlish playfulness is gone, she is a woman steeled in grief.*)

Kate (*for the thousandth time*). Helen.

(*She is down the steps at once to them, seizing* Helen's *wrists and lifting her off* Martha; Martha *runs off in tears and screams for momma, with* Percy *after her.*)

Let me have those scissors.

(*Meanwhile the family inside is alerted,* Aunt Ev *joining* James *at the window;* Captain Keller *resumes work.*)

James (*blandly*). She only dug Martha's eyes out. Almost dug. It's always almost, no point worrying till it happens, is there?

(*They gaze out, while* Kate *reaches for the scissors in* Helen's *hand. But* Helen *pulls the scissors back, they struggle for them a moment, then* Kate *gives up, lets* Helen *keep them. She tries to draw* Helen *into the house.* Helen *jerks away.* Kate *next goes down on her knees, takes* Helen's *hands gently, and using the scissors like a doll, makes* Helen *caress and cradle them; she points* Helen's *finger housewards.* Helen's *whole body now becomes eager; she surrenders the scissors,* Kate *turns her toward the door and gives her a little push.* Helen *scrambles up and toward the house, and* Kate *rising follows her.*)

Aunt Ev. How does she stand it? Why haven't you seen this Baltimore man? It's not a thing you can let go on and on, like the weather.

James. The weather here doesn't ask permission of me, Aunt Ev. Speak to my father.

Aunt Ev. Arthur. Something ought to be done for that child.

Keller. A refreshing suggestion. What?

(Kate *entering turns* Helen *to* Aunt Ev, *who gives her the towel doll.*)

Aunt Ev. Why, this very famous oculist in Baltimore I wrote you about, what was his name?

Kate. Dr. Chisholm.

Aunt Ev. Yes, I heard lots of cases of blindness people thought couldn't be cured he's cured, he just does wonders. Why don't you write to him?

Keller. I've stopped believing in wonders.

Kate (*rocks the cradle*). I think the Captain will write to him soon. Won't you, Captain?

Keller. No.

James (*lightly*). Good money after bad, or bad after good. Or bad after bad—

Aunt Ev. Well, if it's just a question of money, Arthur, now you're marshal you have this Yankee money. Might as well—

Keller. Not money. The child's been to specialists all over Alabama and Tennessee, if I thought it would do good I'd have her to every fool doctor in the country.

Kate. I think the Captain will write to him soon.

Keller. Katie. How many times can you let them break your heart?

Kate. Any number of times.

(Helen *meanwhile sits on the floor to explore the doll with her fingers, and her hand pauses over the face: this is no face, a blank area of towel, and it troubles her. Her hand searches for features, and taps questioningly for eyes, but no one notices. She then yanks at her Aunt's dress, and taps again vigorously for eyes.*)

Aunt Ev. What, child?

(*Obviously not hearing, Helen commences to go around, from person to person, tapping for eyes, but no one attends or understands.*)

Kate (*no break*). As long as there's the least chance. For her to see. Or hear, or—

Keller. There isn't. Now I must finish here.

Kate. I think, with your permission, Captain, I'd like to write.

Keller. I said no, Katie.

Aunt Ev. Why, writing does no harm, Arthur, only a little bitty letter. To see if he can help her.

Keller. He can't.

Kate. We won't know that to be a fact, Captain, until after you write.

Keller (*rising, emphatic*). Katie, he can't.

(*He collects his papers.*)

James (*facetiously*). Father stands up, that makes it a fact.

Keller. You be quiet! I'm badgered enough here by females without your impudence.

(James *shuts up, makes himself scarce. Helen now is groping among things on* Keller's *desk, and paws his papers to the floor.* Keller *is exasperated.*)

Katie.

(Kate *quickly turns* Helen *away, and retrieves the papers.*)

I might as well try to work in a henyard as in this house—

James (*placating*). You really ought to put her away, Father.

Kate (*staring up*). What?

James. Some asylum. It's the kindest thing.

Aunt Ev. Why, she's your sister, James, not a nobody—

James. Half sister, and half—mentally defective, she can't even keep herself clean. It's not pleasant to see her about all the time.

Kate. Do you dare? Complain of what you *can* see?

Keller (*very annoyed*). This discussion is at an end! I'll thank you not to broach it again, Ev.

(*Silence descends at once.* Helen *gropes her way with the doll, and* Keller *turns back for a final word, explosive.*)

I've done as much as I can bear, I can't give my whole life to it! The house is at sixes and sevens from morning till night over the child, it's time some attention was paid to Mildred here instead!

Kate (*gently dry*). You'll wake her up, Captain.

Keller. I want some peace in the house, I don't care how, but one way we won't have it is by rushing up and down the country every time someone hears of a new quack. I'm as sensible to this affliction as anyone else, it hurts me to look at the girl.

Kate. It was not our affliction I meant you to write about, Captain.

(Helen *is back at* Aunt Ev, *fingering her dress, and yanks two buttons from it.*)

Aunt Ev. Helen! My buttons.

(Helen *pushes the buttons into the doll's face.* Kate *now sees, comes swiftly to kneel, lifts* Helen's *hand to her own eyes in question.*)

Kate. Eyes?

(Helen *nods energetically.*)

She wants the doll to have eyes.

(*Another kind of silence now, while* Kate *takes pins and buttons from the sewing basket and attaches them to the doll as eyes.* Keller *stands, caught, and watches morosely.* Aunt Ev *blinks, and conceals her emotion by inspecting her dress.*)

Aunt Ev. My goodness me, I'm not decent.

Kate. She doesn't know better, Aunt Ev. I'll sew them on again.

James. Never learn with everyone letting her do anything she takes it into her mind to—

Keller. You be quiet!

James. What did I say now?

Keller. You talk too much.

James. I was agreeing with you!

Keller. Whatever it was. Deprived child, the least she can have are the little things she wants.

(James, *very wounded, stalks out of the room onto the porch; he remains here, sulking.*)

Aunt Ev (*indulgently*). It's worth a couple of buttons, Kate, look.

(Helen *now has the doll with eyes, and cannot contain herself for joy; she rocks the doll, pats it vigorously, kisses it.*)

This child has more sense than all these men Kellers, if there's ever any way to reach that mind of hers.

(*But* Helen *suddenly has come upon the cradle, and unhesitatingly overturns it; the swaddled baby tumbles out, and* Captain Keller *barely manages to dive and catch it in time.*)

Keller. *Helen!*

(*All are in commotion, the baby screams, but* Helen *unperturbed is laying her doll in its place.* Kate *on her knees pulls her hands off the cradle, wringing them;* Helen *is bewildered.*)

Kate. Helen, Helen, you're not to do such things, how can I make you understand—

Keller (*hoarsely*). Katie.

Kate. How can I get it into your head, my darling, my poor—

Keller. Katie, some way of teaching her an iota of discipline has to be—

Kate (*flaring*). How can you discipline an afflicted child? Is it her fault?

(Helen's *fingers have fluttered to her Mother's lips, vainly trying to comprehend their movements.*)

Keller. I didn't say it was her fault.

Kate. Then whose? I don't know what to do! How can I teach her, beat her—until she's black and blue?

Keller. It's not safe to let her run around loose. Now

there must be a way of confining her, somehow, so she can't—

Kate. Where, in a cage? She's a growing child, she has to use her limbs!

Keller. Answer me one thing, is it fair to Mildred here?

Kate (*inexorably*). Are you willing to put her away?

(*Now* Helen's *face darkens in the same rage as at herself earlier, and her hand strikes at* Kate's *lips.* Kate *catches her hand again, and* Helen *begins to kick, struggle, twist.*)

Keller. Now what?

Kate. She wants to talk, like—*be* like you and me.

(*She holds* Helen *struggling until we hear from the child her first sound so far, an inarticulate weird noise in her throat such as an animal in a trap might make; and* Kate *releases her. The second she is free* Helen *blunders away, collides violently with a chair, falls, and sits weeping.* Kate *comes to her, embraces, caresses, soothes her, and buries her own face in her hair, until she can control her voice.*)

Every day she slips further away. And I don't know how to call her back.

Aunt Ev. Oh, I've a mind to take her up to Baltimore myself. If that doctor can't help her, maybe he'll know who can.

Keller (*presently, heavily*). I'll write the man, Katie.

(*He stands with the baby in his clasp, staring at* Helen's *head, hanging down on* Kate's *arm.*

The lights dim out, except the one on Kate *and* Helen. *In the twilight,* James, Aunt Ev, *and* Keller *move off slowly, formally, in separate directions;* Kate *with* Helen *in her arms remains, motionless, in an image which overlaps into the next scene and fades only when it is well under way.*

Without pause, from the dark down left we hear a man's voice with a Greek accent speaking:)

Anagnos. —who could do nothing for the girl, of course. It was Dr. Bell who thought she might somehow be taught. I have written the family only that a suitable governess, Miss Annie Sullivan, has been found here in Boston—

(The lights begin to come up, down left, on a long table and chair. The table contains equipment for teaching the blind by touch—a small replica of the human skeleton, stuffed animals, models of flowers and plants, piles of books. The chair contains a girl of 20, Annie Sullivan, *with a face which in repose is grave and rather obstinate, and when active is impudent, combative, twinkling with all the life that is lacking in* Helen's, *and handsome; there is a crude vitality to her. Her suitcase is at her knee.* Anagnos, *a stocky bearded man, comes into the light only towards the end of his speech.)*

Anagnos. —and will come. It will no doubt be difficult for you there, Annie. But it has been difficult for you at our school too, hm? Gratifying, yes, when you came to us and could not spell your name, to accomplish so much here in a few years, but always an Irish battle. For independence.

(He studies Annie, *humorously; she does not open her eyes.)*

This is my last time to counsel you, Annie, and you do lack some—by some I mean *all*—what, tact or talent to bend. To others. And what has saved you on more than one occasion here at Perkins is that there was nowhere to expel you to. Your eyes hurt?

Annie. My ears, Mr. Anagnos.

(And now she has opened her eyes; they are inflamed, vague, slightly crossed, clouded by the granular growth of

trachoma, and she often keeps them closed to shut out the pain of light.)

Anagnos (severely). Nowhere but back to Tewksbury, where children learn to be saucy. Annie, I know how dreadful it was there, but that battle is dead and done with, why not let it stay buried?

Annie (cheerily). I think God must owe me a resurrection.

Anagnos (a bit shocked). What?

Annie (taps her brow). Well, He keeps digging up that battle!

Anagnos. That is not a proper thing to say, Annie. It is what I mean.

Annie (meekly). Yes. But I know what I'm like, what's this child like?

Anagnos. Like?

Annie. Well— Bright or dull, to start off.

Anagnos. No one knows. And if she is dull, you have no patience with this?

Annie. Oh, in grownups you have to, Mr. Anagnos. I mean in children it just seems a little—precocious, can I use that word?

Anagnos. Only if you can spell it.

Annie. Premature. So I hope at least she's a bright one.

Anagnos. Deaf, blind, mute—who knows? She is like a little safe, locked, that no one can open. Perhaps there is a treasure inside.

Annie. Maybe it's empty, too?

Anagnos. Possible. I should warn you, she is much given to tantrums.

Annie. Means something is inside. Well, so am I, if I believe all I hear. Maybe you should warn *them*.

Anagnos (*frowns*). Annie. I wrote them no word of your history. You will find yourself among strangers now, who know nothing of it.

Annie. Well, we'll keep them in a state of blessed ignorance.

Anagnos. Perhaps *you* should tell it?

Annie (*bristling*). Why? I have enough trouble with people who don't know.

Anagnos. So they will understand. When you have trouble.

Annie. The only time I have trouble is when I'm right.

(*But she is amused at herself, as is* Anagnos.)

Is it my fault it's so often? I won't give them trouble, Mr. Anagnos, I'll be so ladylike they won't notice I've come.

Anagnos. Annie, be—humble. It is not as if you have so many offers to pick and choose. You will need their affection, working with this child.

Annie (*humorously*). I hope I won't need their pity.

Anagnos. Oh, we can all use some pity.

(*Crisply*)

So. You are no longer our pupil, we throw you into the world, a teacher. *If* the child can be taught. No one expects you to work miracles, even for twenty-five dollars a month. Now, in this envelope a loan, for the railroad, which you will repay me when you have a bank account. But in this box, a gift. With our love.

(Annie *opens the small box he extends, and sees a garnet ring. She looks up, blinking, and down.*)

I think other friends are ready to say goodbye.

(*He moves as though to open doors.*)

Annie. Mr. Anagnos.

(*Her voice is trembling.*)

Dear Mr. Anagnos, I—

(*But she swallows over getting the ring on her finger, and cannot continue until she finds a woebegone joke.*)

Well, what should I say, I'm an ignorant opinionated girl, and everything I am I owe to you?

Anagnos (*smiles*). That is only half true, Annie.

Annie. Which half? I crawled in here like a drowned rat, I thought I died when Jimmie died, that I'd never again—come alive. Well, you say with love so easy, and I haven't *loved* a soul since and I never will, I suppose, but this place gave me more than my eyes back. Or taught me how to spell, which I'll never learn anyway, but with all the fights and the trouble I've been here it taught me what help is, and how to live again, and I don't want to say goodbye. Don't open the door, I'm crying.

Anagnos (*gently*). They will not see.

(*He moves again as though opening doors, and in comes a group of girls, 8-year-olds to 17-year-olds; as they walk we see they are blind. Anagnos shepherds them in with a hand.*)

A child. Annie?

Annie (*her voice cheerful*). Here, Beatrice.

(*As soon as they locate her voice they throng joyfully to her, speaking all at once; Annie is down on her knees to the smallest, and the following are the more intelligible fragments in the general hubbub.*)

Children. There's a present. We brought you a going-away present, Annie!

Annie. Oh, now you shouldn't have—

Children. We did, we did, where's the present?

Smallest Child (*mournfully*). Don't go, Annie, away.

Children. Alice has it. Alice! Where's Alice? Here I am! Where? Here!

(*An arm is aloft out of the group, waving a present; Annie reaches for it.*)

Annie. I have it. I have it, everybody, should I open it?

Children. Open it! Everyone be quiet! Do, Annie! She's opening it. Ssh!

(*A settling of silence while Annie unwraps it. The present is a pair of smoked glasses, and she stands still.*)

Is it open, Annie?

Annie. It's open.

Children. It's for your eyes, Annie. Put them on, Annie! 'Cause Mrs. Hopkins said your eyes hurt since the operation. And she said you're going where the sun is *fierce*.

Annie. I'm putting them on now.

Smallest Child (*mournfully*). Don't go, Annie, where the sun is fierce.

Children. Do they fit all right?

Annie. Oh, they fit just fine.

Children. Did you put them on? Are they pretty, Annie?

Annie. Oh, my eyes feel hundreds of percent better already, and pretty, why, do you know how I look in them? Splendiloquent. Like a race horse!

Children (*delighted*). There's another present! Beatrice! We have a present for Helen, too! Give it to her, Beatrice. Here, Annie!

(*This present is an elegant doll, with movable eyelids and a momma sound.*)

It's for Helen. And we took up a collection to buy it. And Laura dressed it.

Annie. It's beautiful!

Children. So don't forget, you be sure to give it to Helen from us, Annie!

Annie. I promise it will be the first thing I give her. If I don't keep it for myself, that is, you know I can't be trusted with dolls!

Smallest Child (*mournfully*). Don't go, Annie, to her.

Annie (*her arm around her*). Sarah, dear. I don't *want* to go.

Smallest Child. Then why are you going?

Annie (*gently*). Because I'm a big girl now, and big girls have to earn a living. It's the only way I can. But if you don't smile for me first, what I'll just have to do is—

(*She pauses, inviting it.*)

Smallest Child. What?

Annie. Put *you* in my suitcase, instead of this doll. And take *you* to Helen in Alabama!

(*This strikes the children as very funny, and they begin to laugh and tease the smallest child, who after a moment does smile for Annie.*)

Anagnos (*then*). Come, children. We must get the trunk into the carriage and Annie into her train, or no one will go to Alabama. Come, come.

(*He shepherds them out and Annie is left alone on her knees with the doll in her lap. She reaches for her suitcase, and by a subtle change in the color of the light, we go with her thoughts into another time. We hear a boy's voice whispering; perhaps we see shadowy intimations of these speakers in the background.*)

Boy's voice. Where we goin', Annie?

Annie (*in dread*). Jimmie.

Boy's voice. Where we goin'?

Annie. I said—I'm takin' care of you—

Boy's voice. Forever and ever?

Man's voice (*impersonal*). Annie Sullivan, aged nine, virtually blind. James Sullivan, aged seven—What's the matter with your leg, Sonny?

Annie. Forever and ever.

Man's voice. Can't he walk without that crutch?

(*Annie shakes her head, and does not stop shaking it.*)

Girl goes to the women's ward. Boy to the men's.

Boy's voice (*in terror*). Annie! Annie, don't let them take me—Annie!

Anagnos (*offstage*). Annie! Annie?

(*But this voice is real, in the present, and Annie comes up out of her horror, clearing her head with a final shake; the lights begin to pick out* Kate *in the Keller house, as* Annie *in a bright tone calls back.)*

Annie. Coming!

(This word catches Kate, *who stands half turned and attentive to it, almost as though hearing it. Meanwhile* Annie *turns and hurries out, lugging the suitcase.*

The room dims out; the sound of railroad wheels begins from off left, and maintains itself in a constant rhythm underneath the following scene; the remaining lights have come up on the Keller homestead. James *is lounging on the porch, waiting. In the upper bedroom which is to be* Annie's, Helen *is alone, puzzledly exploring, fingering and smelling things, the curtains, empty drawers in the bureau, water in the pitcher by the washbasin, fresh towels on the bedstead. Downstairs in the family room* Kate *turning to a mirror hastily adjusts her bonnet, watched by a Negro servant in an apron,* Viney.)

Viney. Let Mr. Jimmy go by hisself, you been pokin' that garden all day, you ought to rest your feet.

Kate. I can't wait to see her, Viney.

Viney. Maybe she ain't gone be on this train neither.

Kate. Maybe she is.

Viney. And maybe she ain't.

Kate. And maybe she is. Where's Helen?

Viney. She upstairs, smellin' around. She know somethin' funny's goin' on.

Kate. Let her have her supper as soon as Mildred's in bed, and tell Captain Keller when he comes that we'll be delayed tonight.

Viney. Again.

Kate. I don't think we need say *again*. Simply delayed will do.

(*She runs upstairs to Annie's room,* Viney *speaking after her.*)

Viney. I mean that's what he gone say. "What, again?"

(Viney *works at setting the table. Upstairs* Kate *stands in the doorway, watching* Helen's *groping explorations.*)

Kate. Yes, we're expecting someone. Someone for my Helen.

(Helen *happens upon her skirt, clutches her leg;* Kate *in a tired dismay kneels to tidy her hair and soiled pinafore.*)

Oh, dear, this was clean not an hour ago.

(Helen *feels her bonnet, shakes her head darkly, and tugs to get it off.* Kate *retains it with one hand, diverts* Helen *by opening her other hand under her nose.*)

Here. For while I'm gone.

(Helen *sniffs, reaches, and pops something into her mouth, while* Kate *speaks a bit guiltily.*)

I don't think one peppermint drop will spoil your supper.

(*She gives* Helen *a quick kiss, evades her hands, and hurries downstairs again. Meanwhile* Captain Keller *has entered the yard from around the rear of the house, newspaper under arm, cleaning off and munching on some radishes; he sees* James *lounging at the porch post.*)

Keller. Jimmie?

James (*unmoving*). Sir?

Keller (*eyes him*). You don't look dressed for anything useful, boy.

James. I'm not. It's for Miss Sullivan.

Keller. Needn't keep holding up that porch, we have wooden posts for that. I asked you to see that those strawberry plants were moved this evening.

James. I'm moving your—Mrs. Keller, instead. To the station.

Keller (*heavily*). Mrs. Keller. Must you always speak of her as though you haven't met the lady?

(Kate *comes out on the porch, and* James *inclines his head.*)

James (*ironic*). Mother.

(He *starts off the porch, but sidesteps* Keller's *glare like a blow.*)

I said mother!

Kate. Captain.

Keller. Evening, my dear.

Kate. We're off to meet the train, Captain. Supper will be a trifle delayed tonight.

Keller. What, again?

Kate (*backing out*). With your permission, Captain?

(And they are gone. Keller *watches them offstage, morosely.*

Upstairs Helen *meanwhile has groped for her mother, touched her cheek in a meaningful gesture, waited, touched her cheek, waited, then found the open door, and made her way down. Now she comes into the family room, touches her cheek again;* Viney *regards her.*)

Viney. What you want, honey, your momma?

(Helen *touches her cheek again.* Viney *goes to the side-board, gets a tea-cake, gives it into* Helen's *hand;* Helen *pops it into her mouth.*)

Guess one little tea-cake ain't gone ruin your appetite.

(*She turns* Helen *toward the door.* Helen *wanders out onto the porch, as* Keller *comes up the steps. Her hands encounter him, and she touches her cheek again, waits.*)

Keller. She's gone.

(*He is awkward with her; when he puts his hand on her head, she pulls away.* Keller *stands regarding her, heavily.*)

She's gone, my son and I don't get along, you don't know I'm your father, no one likes me, and supper's delayed.

(Helen *touches her cheek, waits.* Keller *fishes in his pocket.*)

Here. I brought you some stick candy, one nibble of sweets can't do any harm.

(*He gives her a large stick candy;* Helen *falls to it.* Viney *peers out the window.*)

Viney (*reproachfully*). Cap'n Keller, now how'm I gone get her to eat her supper you fill her up with that trash?

Keller (*roars*). Tend to your work!

(Viney *beats a rapid retreat.* Keller *thinks better of it, and tries to get the candy away from* Helen, *but* Helen *hangs on to it; and when* Keller *pulls, she gives his leg a kick.* Keller *hops about,* Helen *takes refuge with the candy down behind the pump, and* Keller *then irately flings his newspaper on the porch floor, stamps into the house past* Viney *and disappears.*

The lights half dim on the homestead, where Viney *and* Helen *going about their business soon find their way off. Meanwhile, the railroad sounds off left have mounted in a crescendo to a climax typical of a depot at arrival time, the lights come up on stage left, and we see a suggestion of a station. Here* Annie *in her smoked glasses and disarrayed by travel is waiting with her suitcase, while* James *walks to meet her; she has a battered paper-bound book, which is a Perkins report, under her arm.*)

James (*coolly*). Miss Sullivan?

Annie (*cheerily*). Here! At last, I've been on trains so many days I thought they must be backing up every time I dozed off—

James. I'm James Keller.

Annie. James?

(*The name stops her.*)

I had a brother Jimmie. Are you Helen's?

James. I'm only half a brother. You're to be her governess?

Annie (*lightly*). Well. Try!

James (*eyeing her*). You look like half a governess.

(Kate *enters.* Annie *stands moveless, while* James *takes her suitcase.* Kate's *gaze on her is doubtful, troubled.*)

Mrs. Keller, Miss Sullivan.

(Kate *takes her hand.*)

Kate (*simply*). We've met every train for two days.

(Annie *looks at* Kate's *face, and her good humor comes back.*)

Annie. I changed trains every time they stopped, the man who sold me that ticket ought to be tied to the tracks—

James. You have a trunk, Miss Sullivan?

Annie. Yes.

(*She passes* James *a claim check, and he bears the suitcase out behind them.* Annie *holds the battered book.* Kate *is studying her face, and* Annie *returns the gaze; this is a mutual appraisal, southern gentlewoman and working-class Irish girl, and* Annie *is not quite comfortable under it.*)

You didn't bring Helen, I was hoping you would.

Kate. No, she's home.

(*A pause.* Annie *tries to make ladylike small talk, though her energy now and then erupts; she catches herself up whenever she hears it.*)

Annie. You—live far from town, Mrs. Keller?

Kate. Only a mile.

Annie. Well, I suppose I can wait one more mile. But don't be surprised if I get out to push the horse!

Kate. Helen's waiting for you, too. There's been such a bustle in the house, she expects something, heaven knows what.

(*Now she voices part of her doubt, not as such, but* Annie *understands it.*)

I expected—a desiccated spinster. You're very young.

Annie (*resolutely*). Oh, you should have seen me when I left Boston. I got much older on this trip.

Kate. I mean, to teach anyone as difficult as Helen.

Annie. *I* mean to try. They can't put you in jail for trying!

Kate. Is it possible, even? To teach a deaf-blind child *half* of what an ordinary child learns—has that ever been done?

Annie. Half?

Kate. A tenth.

Annie (*reluctantly*). No.

(Kate's *face loses its remaining hope, still appraising her youth.*)

Dr. Howe did wonders, but—an ordinary child? No, never. But then I thought when I was going over his reports—

(*She indicates the one in her hand.*)

—he never treated them like ordinary children. More like—eggs everyone was afraid would break.

Kate (*a pause*). May I ask how old you are?

Annie. Well, I'm not in my teens, you know! I'm twenty.

Kate. All of twenty.

(Annie *takes the bull by the horns, valiantly.*)

Annie. Mrs. Keller, don't lose heart just because I'm not on my last legs. I have three big advantages over Dr. Howe that money couldn't buy for you. One is his work behind me, I've read every word he wrote about it and he wasn't exactly what you'd call a man of few words. Another is to *be* young, why, I've got energy to do anything. The third is, I've been blind.

(*But it costs her something to say this.*)

Kate (*quietly*). Advantages.

Annie (*wry*). Well, some have the luck of the Irish, some do not.

(Kate *smiles; she likes her.*)

Kate. What will you try to teach her first?

Annie. First, last, and—in between, language.

Kate. Language.

Annie. Language is to the mind more than light is to the eye. Dr. Howe said that.

Kate. Language.

(*She shakes her head.*)

We can't get through to teach her to sit still. You *are* young, despite your years, to have such—confidence. Do you, inside?

(Annie *studies her face; she likes her, too.*)

Annie. No, to tell you the truth I'm as shaky inside as a baby's rattle!

(*They smile at each other, and* Kate *pats her hand.*)

Kate. Don't be.

(James *returns to usher them off.*)

We'll do all we can to help, and to make you feel at home. Don't think of us as strangers, Miss Annie.

Annie (*cheerily*). Oh, strangers aren't so strange to me. I've known them all my life!

(Kate *smiles again,* Annie *smiles back, and they precede* James *offstage.*

The lights dim on them, having simultaneously risen full on the house; Viney *has already entered the family room, taken a water pitcher, and come out and down to the pump. She pumps real water. As she looks offstage, we hear the clop of hoofs, a carriage stopping, and voices.*)

Viney. Cap'n Keller! Cap'n Keller, they comin'!

(She goes back into the house, as Keller *comes out on the porch to gaze.)*

She sure 'nuff came, Cap'n.

(Keller descends, and crosses toward the carriage; this conversation begins offstage and moves on.)

Keller *(very courtly).* Welcome to Ivy Green, Miss Sullivan. I take it you are Miss Sullivan—

Kate. My husband, Miss Annie, Captain Keller.

Annie *(her best behavior).* Captain, how do you do.

Keller. A pleasure to see you, at last. I trust you had an agreeable journey?

Annie. Oh, I had several! When did this country get so big?

James. Where would you like the trunk, father?

Keller. Where Miss Sullivan can get at it, I imagine.

Annie. Yes, please. Where's Helen?

Keller. In the hall, Jimmie—

Kate. We've put you in the upstairs corner room, Miss Annie, if there's any breeze at all this summer, you'll feel it—

(In the house the setter Belle flees into the family room, pursued by Helen with groping hands; the dog doubles back out the same door, and Helen still groping for her makes her way out to the porch; she is messy, her hair tumbled, her pinafore now ripped, her shoelaces untied. Keller acquires the suitcase, and Annie gets her hands on it too, though still endeavoring to live up to the general air of propertied manners.)

Keller. *And* the suitcase—

Annie (*pleasantly*). I'll take the suitcase, thanks.

Keller. Not at all, I have it, Miss Sullivan.

Annie. I'd like it.

Keller (*gallantly*). I couldn't think of it, Miss Sullivan. You'll find in the south we—

Annie. Let me.

Keller. —view women as the flowers of civiliza—

Annie (*impatiently*). I've got something in it for Helen!

(*She tugs it free; Keller stares.*)

Thank you. When do I see her?

Kate. There. There is Helen.

(*Annie turns, and sees Helen on the porch. A moment of silence. Then Annie begins across the yard to her, lugging her suitcase.*)

Keller (*sotto voce*). Katie—

(*Kate silences him with a hand on his arm. When Annie finally reaches the porch steps she stops, contemplating Helen for a last moment before entering her world. Then she drops the suitcase on the porch with intentional heaviness, Helen starts with the jar, and comes to grope over it. Annie puts forth her hand, and touches Helen's. Helen at once grasps it, and commences to explore it, like reading a face. She moves her hand on to Annie's forearm, and dress; and Annie brings her face within reach of Helen's fingers, which travel over it, quite without timidity, until they encounter and push aside the smoked glasses. Annie's gaze is grave, unpitying, very attentive. She puts her hands on Helen's arms, but Helen at once pulls away, and they confront each other with a distance between. Then Helen returns to the suitcase, tries to open it, cannot. Annie points Helen's hand overhead. Helen pulls away, tries to open the suitcase again;* Annie *points her hand overhead again.* Helen *points overhead, a question, and* Annie, *drawing* Helen's *hand to her own face, nods.* Helen *now begins tugging the suitcase toward the door, when* Annie *tries to take it from her, she fights her off and backs through the doorway with it.* Annie *stands a moment, then follows her in, and together they get the suitcase up the steps into* Annie's *room.)*

Kate. Well?

Keller. She's very rough, Katie.

Kate. I like her, Captain.

Keller. Certainly rear a peculiar kind of young woman in the north. How old is she?

Kate (*vaguely*). Ohh— Well, she's not in her teens, you know.

Keller. She's only a child. What's her family like, shipping her off alone this far?

Kate. I couldn't learn. She's very closemouthed about some things.

Keller. Why does she wear those glasses? I like to see a person's eyes when I talk to—

Kate. For the sun. She was blind.

Keller. Blind.

Kate. She's had nine operations on her eyes. One just before she left.

Keller. Blind, good heavens, do they expect one blind child to teach another? Has she experience at least, how long did she teach there?

Kate. She was a pupil.

Keller (*heavily*). Katie, Katie. This is her first position?

Kate (*bright voice*). She was valedictorian—

Keller. Here's a houseful of grownups can't cope with the child, how can an inexperienced half-blind Yankee schoolgirl manage her?

(James *moves in with the trunk on his shoulder.*)

James (*easily*). Great improvement. Now we have two of them to look after.

Keller. You look after those strawberry plants!

(James *stops with the trunk.* Keller *turns from him without another word, and marches off.*)

James. Nothing I say is right.

Kate. Why say anything?

(*She calls.*)

Don't be long, Captain, we'll have supper right away—

(*She goes into the house, and through the rear door of the family room.* James *trudges in with the trunk, takes it up the steps to Annie's room, and sets it down outside the door. The lights elsewhere dim somewhat.*

Meanwhile, inside, Annie *has given* Helen *a key; while* Annie *removes her bonnet,* Helen *unlocks and opens the suitcase. The first thing she pulls out is a voluminous shawl. She fingers it until she perceives what it is; then she wraps it around her, and acquiring Annie's bonnet and smoked glasses as well, dons the lot: the shawl swamps her, and the bonnet settles down upon the glasses, but she stands before a mirror cocking her head to one side, then to the other, in a mockery of adult action.* Annie *is amused, and talks to her as one might to a kitten, with no trace of company manners.*)

Annie. All the trouble I went to and that's how I look?

(Helen *then comes back to the suitcase, gropes for more, lifts out a pair of female drawers.*)

Oh, no. Not the drawers!

(*But* Helen *discarding them comes to the elegant doll. Her fingers explore its features, and when she raises it and finds its eyes open and close, she is at first startled, then delighted. She picks it up, taps its head vigorously, taps her own chest, and nods questioningly.* Annie *takes her finger, points it to the doll, points it to* Helen, *and touching it to her own face, also nods.* Helen *sits back on her heels, clasps the doll to herself, and rocks it.* Annie *studies her, still in bonnet and smoked glasses like a caricature of herself, and addresses her humorously.*)

All right, Miss O'Sullivan. Let's begin with doll.

(*She takes* Helen's *hand; in her palm* Annie's *forefinger points, thumb holding her other fingers clenched.*)

D.

(*Her thumb next holds all her fingers clenched, touching* Helen's *palm.*)

O.

(*Her thumb and forefinger extend.*)

L.

(*Same contact repeated.*)

L.

(*She puts* Helen's *hand to the doll.*)

Doll.

James. You spell pretty well.

(Annie *in one hurried move gets the drawers swiftly back into the suitcase, the lid banged shut, and her head turned, to see* James *leaning in the doorway.*)

Finding out if she's ticklish? She is.

(Annie *regards him stonily, but* Helen *after a scowling moment tugs at her hand again, imperious.* Annie *repeats the letters, and* Helen *interrupts her fingers in the middle, feeling each of them, puzzled.* Annie *touches* Helen's *hand to the doll, and begins spelling into it again.*)

James. What is it, a game?

Annie (*curtly*). An alphabet.

James. Alphabet?

Annie. For the deaf.

(Helen *now repeats the finger movements in air, exactly, her head cocked to her own hand, and* Annie's *eyes suddenly gleam.*)

Ho. How *bright* she is!

James. You think she knows what she's doing?

(*He takes* Helen's *hand, to throw a meaningless gesture into it; she repeats this one too.*)

She imitates everything, she's a monkey.

Annie (*very pleased*). Yes, she's a bright little monkey, all right.

(*She takes the doll from* Helen, *and reaches for her hand;* Helen *instantly grabs the doll back.* Annie *takes it again, and* Helen's *hand next, but* Helen *is incensed now; when* Annie *draws her hand to her face to shake her head no, then tries to spell to her,* Helen *slaps at* Annie's *face.* Annie *grasps* Helen *by both arms, and swings her into a chair, holding her pinned there, kicking, while glasses, doll, bonnet fly in various directions.* James *laughs.*)

James. She wants her doll back.

Annie. When she spells it.

James. Spell, she doesn't know the thing has a name, even.

Annie. Of course not, who expects her to, now? All I want is her fingers to learn the letters.

James. Won't mean anything to her.

(Annie *gives him a look. She then tries to form* Helen's *fingers into the letters, but* Helen *swings a haymaker instead, which* Annie *barely ducks, at once pinning her down again.*)

Doesn't like that alphabet, Miss Sullivan. You invent it yourself?

(Helen *is now in a rage, fighting tooth and nail to get out of the chair, and* Annie *answers while struggling and dodging her kicks.*)

Annie. Spanish monks under a—vow of silence. Which I wish *you'd* take!

(*And suddenly releasing* Helen's *hands, she comes and shuts the door in* James's *face.* Helen *drops to the floor, groping around for the doll.* Annie *looks around desperately, sees her purse on the bed, rummages in it, and comes up with a battered piece of cake wrapped in newspaper; with her foot she moves the doll deftly out of the way of* Helen's *groping, and going on her knee she lets* Helen *smell the cake. When* Helen *grabs for it,* Annie *removes the cake and spells quickly into the reaching hand.*)

Cake. From Washington up north, it's the best I can do.

(Helen's *hand waits, baffled.* Annie *repeats it.*)

C, a, k, e. Do what my fingers do, never mind what it means.

(*She touches the cake briefly to* Helen's *nose, pats her hand, presents her own hand.* Helen *spells the letters rapidly back.* Annie *pats her hand enthusiastically, and gives her the cake;* Helen *crams it into her mouth with both hands.* Annie *watches her, with humor.)*

Get it down fast, maybe I'll steal that back too. Now.

(She takes the doll, touches it to Helen's *nose, and spells again into her hand.)*

D, o, l, l. Think it over.

(Helen thinks it over, while Annie *presents her own hand. Then* Helen *spells three letters.* Annie *waits a second, then completes the word for* Helen *in her palm.)*

L.

(She hands over the doll, and Helen *gets a good grip on its leg.)*

Imitate now, understand later. End of the first les—

(She never finishes, because Helen *swings the doll with a furious energy, it hits* Annie *squarely in the face, and she falls back with a cry of pain, her knuckles up to her mouth.* Helen *waits, tensed for further combat. When* Annie *lowers her knuckles she looks at blood on them; she works her lips, gets to her feet, finds the mirror, and bares her teeth at herself. Now she is furious herself.)*

You little wretch, no one's taught you *any* manners? I'll—

(But rounding from the mirror she sees the door slam, Helen *and the doll are on the outside, and* Helen *is turning the key in the lock.* Annie *darts over, to pull the knob, the door is locked fast. She yanks it again.)*

Helen! Helen, let me out of—

(She bats her brow at the folly of speaking, but James, *now*

downstairs, hears her and turns to see Helen *with the key and doll groping her way down the steps.* James *takes in the whole situation, makes a move to intercept* Helen, *but then changes his mind, lets her pass, and amusedly follows her out onto the porch. Upstairs* Annie *meanwhile rattles the knob, kneels, peers through the keyhole, gets up. She goes to the window, looks down, frowns.* James *from the yard sings gaily up to her:)*

James.

Buffalo girl, are you coming out tonight,
Coming out tonight,
Coming out—

(He drifts back into the house. Annie *takes a handkerchief, nurses her mouth, stands in the middle of the room, staring at door and window in turn, and so catches sight of herself in the mirror, her cheek scratched, her hair dishevelled, her handkerchief bloody, her face disgusted with herself. She addresses the mirror, with some irony.)*

Annie. Don't worry. They'll find you, you're not lost. Only out of place.

(But she coughs, spits something into her palm, and stares at it, outraged.)

And toothless.

(She winces.)

Oo! It hurts.

(She pours some water into the basin, dips the handkerchief, and presses it to her mouth. Standing there, bent over the basin in pain—with the rest of the set dim and unreal, and the lights upon her taking on the subtle color of the past—she hears again, as do we, the faraway voices, and slowly she lifts her head to them; the boy's voice is the same, the others are cracked old crones in a nightmare, and perhaps we see their shadows.)

Boy's voice. It hurts. Annie, it hurts.

First Crone's voice. Keep that brat shut up, can't you, girlie, how's a body to get any sleep in this damn ward?

Boy's voice. It hurts. It hurts.

Second Crone's voice. Shut up, you!

Boy's voice. Annie, when are we goin' home? You promised!

Annie. Jimmie—

Boy's voice. Forever and ever, you said forever—

(Annie drops *the handkerchief, averts to the window, and is arrested there by the next cry.*)

Annie? Annie, you there? Annie! It *hurts!*

Third Crone's voice. Grab him, he's fallin'!

Boy's voice. *Annie!*

Doctor's voice (*a pause, slowly*). Little girl. Little girl, I must tell you your brother will be going on a—

(*But* Annie *claps her hands to her ears, to shut this out, there is instant silence.*

As the lights bring the other areas in again, James *goes to the steps to listen for any sound from upstairs.* Keller *re-entering from left crosses toward the house; he passes* Helen *en route to her retreat under the pump.* Kate *re-enters the rear door of the family room, with flowers for the table.*)

Kate. Supper is ready, Jimmie, will you call your father?

James. Certainly.

(*But he calls up the stairs, for* Annie's *benefit.*)

Father! Supper!

Keller (*at the door*). No need to shout, I've been cooling my heels for an hour. Sit down.

James. Certainly.

Keller. Viney!

(Viney *backs in with a roast, while they get settled around the table.*)

Viney. Yes, Cap'n, right here.

Kate. Mildred went directly to sleep, Viney?

Viney. Oh yes, that babe's a angel.

Kate. And Helen had a good supper?

Viney (*vaguely*). I dunno, Miss Kate, somehow she didn't have much of a appetite tonight—

Kate (*a bit guilty*). Oh. Dear.

Keller (*hastily*). Well, now. Couldn't say the same for my part, I'm famished. Katie, your plate.

Kate (*looking*). But where is Miss Annie?

(*A silence.*)

James (*pleasantly*). In her room.

Keller. In her room? Doesn't she know hot food must be eaten hot? Go bring her down at once, Jimmie.

James (*rises*). Certainly. I'll get a ladder.

Keller (*stares*). What?

James. I'll need a ladder. Shouldn't take me long.

Kate (*stares*). What shouldn't take you—

Keller. Jimmie, do as I say! Go upstairs at once and tell Miss Sullivan supper is getting cold—

James. She's locked in her room.

Keller. Locked in her—

Kate. What on earth are you—

James. Helen locked her in and made off with the key.

Kate (*rising*). And you sit here and say nothing?

James. Well, everyone's been telling me not to say anything.

(*He goes serenely out and across the yard, whistling. Keller thrusting up from his chair makes for the stairs.*)

Kate. Viney, look out in back for Helen. See if she has that key.

Viney. Yes, Miss Kate.

(Viney *goes out the rear door.*)

Keller (*calling down*). She's out by the pump!

(Kate *goes out on the porch after* Helen, *while* Keller *knocks on* Annie's *door, then rattles the knob, imperiously.*)

Miss Sullivan! Are you in there?

Annie. Oh, I'm in here, all right.

Keller. Is there no key on your side?

Annie (*with some asperity*). Well, if there was a key in here, *I* wouldn't be in here. Helen took it, the only thing on my side is me.

Keller. Miss Sullivan. I—

(*He tries, but cannot hold it back.*)

Not in the house ten minutes, I don't see *how* you
managed it!

(*He stomps downstairs again, while* Annie *mutters to
herself.*)

Annie. And even I'm not on my side.

Keller (*roaring*). Viney!

Viney (*reappearing*). Yes, Cap'n?

Keller. Put that meat back in the oven!

(Viney *bears the roast off again, while* Keller *strides out onto
the porch.* Kate *is with* Helen *at the pump, opening her
hands.*)

Kate. She has no key.

Keller. Nonsense, she must have the key. Have you
searched in her pockets?

Kate. Yes. She doesn't have it.

Keller. Katie, she must have the key.

Kate. Would you prefer to search her yourself,
Captain?

Keller. No, I would not prefer to search her! She
almost took my kneecap off this evening, when I
tried merely to—

(James *reappears carrying a long ladder, with* Percy *running
after him to be in on things.*)

Take that ladder back!

James. Certainly.

(*He turns around with it.* Martha *comes skipping around the
upstage corner of the house to be in on things, accompa-
nied by the setter* Belle.)

Kate. She could have hidden the key.

Keller. Where?

Kate. Anywhere. Under a stone. In the flower beds. In the grass—

Keller. Well, I can't plow up the entire grounds to find a missing key! Jimmie!

James. Sir?

Keller. Bring me a ladder!

James. Certainly.

(Viney *comes around the downstage side of the house to be in on things; she has* Mildred *over her shoulder, bleating.* Keller *places the ladder against Annie's window and mounts.* Annie *meanwhile is running about making herself presentable, washing the blood off her mouth, straightening her clothes, tidying her hair. Another Negro servant enters to gaze in wonder, increasing the gathering ring of spectators.*)

Kate (*sharply*). What is Mildred doing up?

Viney. Cap'n woke her, ma'am, all that hollerin'.

Keller. Miss Sullivan!

(Annie *comes to the window, with as much air of gracious normality as she can manage;* Keller *is at the window.*)

Annie (*brightly*). Yes, Captain Keller?

Keller. Come out!

Annie. I don't see how I can. There isn't room.

Keller. I intend to carry you. Climb onto my shoulder and hold tight.

Annie. Oh, no. It's—very chivalrous of you, but I'd really prefer to—

Keller. Miss Sullivan, follow instructions! I will not have you also tumbling out of our windows.

(Annie *obeys, with some misgivings.*)

I hope this is not a sample of what we may expect from you. In the way of simplifying the work of looking after Helen.

Annie. Captain Keller, I'm perfectly able to go down a ladder under my own—

Keller. I doubt it, Miss Sullivan. Simply hold onto my neck.

(*He begins down with her, while the spectators stand in a wide and somewhat awe-stricken circle, watching.* Keller *half-misses a rung, and* Annie *grabs at his whiskers.*)

My *neck*, Miss Sullivan!

Annie. I'm sorry to inconvenience you this way—

Keller. No inconvenience, other than having that door taken down and the lock replaced, if we fail to find that key.

Annie. Oh, I'll look everywhere for it.

Keller. Thank you. Do not look in any rooms that can be locked. There.

(*He stands her on the ground.* James *applauds.*)

Annie. Thank you very much.

(*She smooths her skirt, looking as composed and ladylike as possible.* Keller *stares around at the spectators.*)

Keller. Go, go, back to your work. What are you looking at here? There's nothing here to look at.

(*They break up, move off.*)

Now would it be possible for us to have supper, like other people?

(*He marches into the house.*)

Kate. Viney, serve supper. I'll put Mildred to sleep.

(*They all go in.* James *is the last to leave, murmuring to* Annie *with a gesture.*)

James. Might as well leave the l, a, d, d, e, r, hm?

(Annie *ignores him, looking at* Helen; James *goes in too. Imperceptibly the lights commence to narrow down.* Annie *and* Helen *are now alone in the yard,* Helen *seated at the pump, where she has been oblivious to it all, a battered little savage, playing with the doll in a picture of innocent contentment.* Annie *comes near, leans against the house, and taking off her smoked glasses, studies her, not without awe. Presently* Helen *rises, gropes around to see if anyone is present,* Annie *evades her hand, and when* Helen *is satisfied she is alone, the key suddenly protrudes out of her mouth. She takes it in her fingers, stands thinking, gropes to the pump, lifts a loose board, drops the key into the well, and hugs herself gleefully.* Annie *stares. But after a moment she shakes her head to herself, she cannot keep the smile from her lips.*)

Annie. You *devil.*

(*Her tone is one of great respect, humor, and acceptance of challenge.*)

You think I'm so easily gotten rid of? You have a thing or two to learn, first. I have nothing else to do.

(*She goes up the steps to the porch, but turns for a final word, almost of warning.*)

And nowhere to go.

(*And presently she moves into the house to the others, as the lights dim down and out, except for the small circle upon* Helen *solitary at the pump, which ends the act.*)

ACT **TWO**

It is evening.

The only room visible in the Keller house is Annie's, *where by lamplight* Annie *in a shawl is at a desk writing a letter; at her bureau* Helen *in her customary unkempt state is tucking her doll in the bottom drawer as a cradle, the contents of which she has dumped out, creating as usual a fine disorder.*

Annie mutters each word as she writes her letter, slowly, her eyes close to and almost touching the page, to follow with difficulty her penwork.

Annie. ". . . and, nobody, here, has, attempted, to, control, her. The, greatest, problem, I, have, is, how, to, discipline, her, without, breaking, her, spirit."

(Resolute voice)

"But, I, shall, insist, on, reasonable, obedience, from, the, start—"

(At which point Helen, *groping about on the desk, knocks over the inkwell.* Annie *jumps up, rescues her letter, rights the inkwell, grabs a towel to stem the spillage, and then wipes at* Helen's *hands;* Helen *as always pulls free, but not until* Annie *first gets three letters into her palm.)*

Ink.

*(*Helen *is enough interested in and puzzled by this spelling that she proffers her hand again; so* Annie *spells and impassively dunks it back in the spillage.)*

Ink. It has a name.

(*She wipes the hand clean, and leads* Helen *to her bureau, where she looks for something to engage her. She finds a sewing card, with needle and thread, and going to her knees, shows* Helen's *hand how to connect one row of holes.*)

Down. Under. Up. And be careful of the needle—

(Helen *gets it, and* Annie *rises.*)

Fine. You keep out of the ink and perhaps I can keep out of—the soup.

(*She returns to the desk, tidies it, and resumes writing her letter, bent close to the page.*)

"These, blots, are, her, handiwork. I—"

(*She is interrupted by a gasp:* Helen *has stuck her finger, and sits sucking at it, darkly. Then with vengeful resolve she seizes her doll, and is about to dash its brains out on the floor when* Annie *diving catches it in one hand, which she at once shakes with hopping pain but otherwise ignores, patiently.*)

All right, let's try temperance.

(*Taking the doll, she kneels, goes through the motion of knocking its head on the floor, spells into* Helen's *hand:*)

Bad, girl.

(*She lets* Helen *feel the grieved expression on her face.* Helen *imitates it. Next she makes* Helen *caress the doll and kiss the hurt spot and hold it gently in her arms, then spells into her hand:*)

Good, girl.

(*She lets* Helen *feel the smile on her face.* Helen *sits with a scowl, which suddenly clears; she pats the doll, kisses it, wreathes her face in a large artificial smile, and bears the doll to the washstand, where she carefully sits it. Annie watches, pleased.)*

Very good girl—

(Whereupon Helen elevates the pitcher and dashes it on the floor instead. Annie leaps to her feet, and stands inarticulate; Helen calmly gropes back to the sewing card and needle.

Annie *manages to achieve self-control. She picks up a fragment or two of the pitcher, sees* Helen *is puzzling over the card, and resolutely kneels to demonstrate it again. She spells into* Helen's *hand.*

Kate *meanwhile coming around the corner with folded sheets on her arm, halts at the doorway and watches them for a moment in silence; she is moved, but level.)*

Kate *(presently).* What are you saying to her?

(Annie glancing up is a bit embarrassed, and rises from the spelling, to find her company manners.)

Annie. Oh, I was just making conversation. Saying it was a sewing card.

Kate. But does that—

(She imitates with her fingers)

—mean that to her?

Annie. No. No, she won't know what spelling is till she knows what a word is.

Kate. Yet you keep spelling to her. Why?

Annie *(cheerily).* I like to hear myself talk!

Kate. The Captain says it's like spelling to the fence post.

Annie (*a pause*). Does he, now.

Kate. Is it?

Annie. No, it's how I watch you talk to Mildred.

Kate. Mildred.

Annie. Any baby. Gibberish, grown-up gibberish, baby-talk gibberish, do they understand one word of it to start? Somehow they begin to. If they hear it, I'm letting Helen hear it.

Kate. Other children are not—impaired.

Annie. Ho, there's nothing impaired in that head, it works like a mousetrap!

Kate (*smiles*). But after a child hears how many words, Miss Annie, a million?

Annie. I guess no mother's ever minded enough to count.

(*She drops her eyes to spell into* Helen's *hand, again indicating the card;* Helen *spells back, and* Annie *is amused.*)

Kate (*too quickly*). What did she spell?

Annie. I spelt card. She spelt cake!

(*She takes in* Kate's *quickness, and shakes her head, gently.*)

No, it's only a finger-game to her, Mrs. Keller. What she has to learn first is that things have names.

Kate. And when will she learn?

Annie. Maybe after a million and one words.

(*They hold each other's gaze;* Kate *then speaks quietly.*)

Kate. I should like to learn those letters, Miss Annie.

Annie (*pleased*). I'll teach you tomorrow morning. That makes only half a million each!

Kate (*then*). It's her bedtime.

(Annie *reaches for the sewing card,* Helen *objects,* Annie *insists, and* Helen *gets rid of* Annie's *hand by jabbing it with the needle.* Annie *gasps, and moves to grip* Helen's *wrist; but* Kate *intervenes with a proffered sweet, and* Helen *drops the card, crams the sweet into her mouth, and scrambles up to search her mother's hands for more.* Annie *nurses her wound, staring after the sweet.*)

I'm sorry, Miss Annie.

Annie (*indignantly*). Why does she get a reward? For stabbing me?

Kate. Well—

(*Then, tiredly*)

We catch our flies with honey, I'm afraid. We haven't the heart for much else, and so many times she simply cannot be compelled.

Annie (*ominous*). Yes. I'm the same way myself.

(Kate *smiles, and leads* Helen *off around the corner.* Annie *alone in her room picks up things and in the act of removing* Helen's *doll gives way to unmannerly temptation: she throttles it. She drops it on her bed, and stands pondering. Then she turns back, sits decisively, and writes again, as the lights dim on her.*)

(*Grimly*)

"The, more, I, think, the, more, certain, I, am, that, obedience, is, the, gateway, through, which, knowledge, enters, the, mind, of, the, child—"

(*On the word "obedience" a shaft of sunlight hits the water pump outside, while* Annie's *voice ends in the dark, followed by a distant cockcrow; daylight comes up over another corner of the sky, with* Viney's *voice heard at once.*)

Viney. Breakfast ready!

(Viney *comes down into the sunlight beam, and pumps a pitcherful of water. While the pitcher is brimming we hear conversation from the dark; the light grows to the family room of the house where all are either entering or already seated at breakfast, with* Keller *and* James *arguing the war.* Helen *is wandering around the table to explore the contents of the other plates. When* Annie *is in her chair, she watches* Helen. Viney *re-enters, sets the pitcher on the table;* Kate *lifts the almost empty biscuit plate with an inquiring look,* Viney *nods and bears it off back, neither of them interrupting the men.* Annie *meanwhile sits with fork quiet, watching* Helen, *who at her mother's plate pokes her hand among some scrambled eggs.* Kate *catches* Annie's *eyes on her, smiles with a wry gesture.* Helen *moves on to* James's *plate, the male talk continuing,* James *deferential and* Keller *overriding.*)

James. —no, but shouldn't we give the devil his due, father? The fact is we lost the South two years earlier when he outthought us behind Vicksburg.

Keller. Outthought is a peculiar word for a butcher.

James. Harness maker, wasn't he?

Keller. I said butcher, his only virtue as a soldier was numbers and he led them to slaughter with no more regard than for so many sheep.

James. But even if in that sense he was a butcher, the fact is he—

Keller. And a drunken one, half the war.

James. Agreed, father. If his own people said he was I can't argue he—

Keller. Well, what is it you find to admire in such a man, Jimmie, the butchery or the drunkenness?

James. Neither, father, only the fact that he beat us.

Keller. He didn't.

James. Is it your contention we won the war, sir?

Keller. He didn't beat us at Vicksburg. We lost Vicksburg because Pemberton gave Bragg five thousand of his cavalry and Loring, whom I knew personally for a nincompoop before you were born, marched away from Champion's Hill with enough men to have held them. We lost Vicksburg by stupidity verging on treason.

James. I would have said we lost Vicksburg because Grant was one thing no Yankee general was before him—

Keller. Drunk? I doubt it.

James. Obstinate.

Keller. Obstinate. Could any of them compare even in that with old Stonewall? If he'd been there we would still have Vicksburg.

James. Well, the butcher simply wouldn't give up, he tried four ways of getting around Vicksburg and on the fifth try he got around. Anyone else would have pulled north and—

Keller. He wouldn't have got around if we'd had a Southerner in command, instead of a half-breed Yankee traitor like Pemberton—

(*While this background talk is in progress,* Helen *is working around the table, ultimately toward* Annie's *plate. She messes with her hands in* James's *plate, then in* Keller's, *both men taking it so for granted they hardly notice. Then* Helen *comes groping with soiled hands past her own plate, to* Annie's; *her hand goes to it, and* Annie, *who has been waiting, deliberately lifts and removes her hand.* Helen

The Miracle Worker   57

gropes again, Annie *firmly pins her by the wrist, and removes her hand from the table.* Helen *thrusts her hands again,* Annie *catches them, and* Helen *begins to flail and make noises; the interruption brings* Keller's *gaze upon them.)*

What's the matter there?

Kate. Miss Annie. You see, she's accustomed to helping herself from our plates to anything she—

Annie (*evenly*). Yes, but *I'm* not accustomed to it.

Keller. No, of course not. Viney!

Kate. Give her something, Jimmie, to quiet her.

James (*blandly*). But her table manners are the best she has. Well.

(He pokes across with a chunk of bacon at Helen's *hand, which* Annie *releases; but* Helen *knocks the bacon away and stubbornly thrusts at* Annie's *plate,* Annie *grips her wrists again, the struggle mounts.)*

Keller. Let her this time, Miss Sullivan, it's the only way we get any adult conversation. If my son's half merits that description.

(He rises.)

I'll get you another plate.

Annie (*gripping* Helen). I have a plate, thank you.

Kate (*calling*). Viney! I'm afraid what Captain Keller says is only too true, she'll persist in this until she gets her own way.

Keller (*at the door*). Viney, bring Miss Sullivan another plate—

Annie (*stonily*). I have a plate, nothing's wrong with the *plate*, I intend to keep it.

(*Silence for a moment, except for* Helen's *noises as she struggles to get loose; the* Kellers *are a bit nonplussed, and* Annie *is too darkly intent on* Helen's *manners to have any thoughts now of her own.*)

James. Ha. You see why they took Vicksburg?

Keller (*uncertainly*). Miss Sullivan. One plate or another is hardly a matter to struggle with a deprived child about.

Annie. Oh, I'd sooner have a more—

(Helen *begins to kick,* Annie *moves her ankles to the opposite side of the chair.*)

—heroic issue myself, I—

Keller. No, I really must insist you—

(Helen *bangs her toe on the chair and sinks to the floor, crying with rage and feigned injury;* Annie *keeps hold of her wrists, gazing down, while* Kate *rises.*)

Now she's hurt herself.

Annie (*grimly*). No, she hasn't.

Keller. Will you please let her hands go?

Kate. Miss Annie, you don't know the child well enough yet, she'll keep—

Annie. I know an ordinary tantrum well enough, when I see one, and a badly spoiled child—

James. Hear, hear.

Keller (*very annoyed*). Miss Sullivan! You would have more understanding of your pupil if you had some pity in you. Now kindly do as I—

Annie. Pity?

(*She releases* Helen *to turn equally annoyed on* Keller *across the table; instantly* Helen *scrambles up and dives at Annie's plate. This time* Annie *intercepts her by pouncing on her wrists like a hawk, and her temper boils.*)

For this *tyrant?* The whole house turns on her whims, is there anything she wants she doesn't get? I'll tell you what I pity, that the sun won't rise and set for her all her life, and every day you're telling her it will, what good will your pity do her when you're under the strawberries, Captain Keller?

Keller (*outraged*). Kate, for the love of heaven will you—

Kate. Miss Annie, please, I don't think it serves to lose our—

Annie. It does you good, that's all. It's less trouble to feel sorry for her than to teach her anything better, isn't it?

Keller. I fail to see where you have taught her anything yet, Miss Sullivan!

Annie. I'll begin this minute, if you'll leave the room, Captain Keller!

Keller (*astonished*). Leave the—

Annie. Everyone, please.

(*She struggles with* Helen, *while* Keller *endeavors to control his voice.*)

Keller. Miss Sullivan, you are here only as a paid teacher. Nothing more, and not to lecture—

Annie. I can't *un*teach her six years of pity if you can't stand up to one tantrum! Old Stonewall, indeed. Mrs. Keller, you promised me help.

Kate. Indeed I did, we truly want to—

Annie. Then leave me alone with her. Now!

Keller (*in a wrath*). Katie, will you come outside with me? At once, please.

(*He marches to the front door.* Kate *and* James *follow him. Simultaneously* Annie *releases* Helen's *wrists, and the child again sinks to the floor, kicking and crying her weird noises;* Annie *steps over her to meet* Viney *coming in the rear doorway with biscuits and a clean plate, surprised at the general commotion.*)

Viney. Heaven sakes—

Annie. Out, please.

(*She backs* Viney *out with one hand, closes the door on her astonished mouth, locks it, and removes the key.* Keller *meanwhile snatches his hat from a rack, and* Kate *follows him down the porch steps.* James *lingers in the doorway to address* Annie *across the room with a bow.*)

James. If it takes all summer, general.

(Annie *comes over to his door in turn, removing her glasses grimly; as* Keller *outside begins speaking,* Annie *closes the door on* James, *locks it, removes the key, and turns with her back against the door to stare ominously at* Helen, *kicking on the floor.*

James *takes his hat from the rack, and going down the porch steps joins* Kate *and* Keller *talking in the yard,* Keller *in a sputter of ire.*)

Keller. This girl, this—cub of a girl—*presumes!* I tell you, I'm of half a mind to ship her back to Boston before the week is out. You can inform her so from me!

Kate (*eyebrows up*). I, Captain?

Keller. She's a *hireling!* Now I want it clear, unless

there's an apology and complete change of manner she goes back on the next train! Will you make that quite clear?

Kate. Where will you be, Captain, while I am making it quite—

Keller. At the office!

(*He begins off left, finds his napkin still in his irate hand, is uncertain with it, dabs his lips with dignity, gets rid of it in a toss to* James, *and marches off.* James *turns to eye* Kate.)

James. Will you?

(Kate's *mouth is set, and* James *studies it lightly.*)

I thought what she said was exceptionally intelligent. I've been saying it for years.

Kate (*not without scorn*). To his face?

(*She comes to relieve him of the white napkin, but reverts again with it.*)

Or will you take it, Jimmie? As a flag?

(James *stalks out, much offended, and* Kate *turning stares across the yard at the house; the lights narrowing down to the following pantomime in the family room leave her motionless in the dark.*

Annie *meanwhile has begun by slapping both keys down on a shelf out of* Helen's *reach; she returns to the table, upstage.* Helen's *kicking has subsided, and when from the floor her hand finds* Annie's *chair empty she pauses.* Annie *clears the table of* Kate's, James's, *and* Keller's *plates; she gets back to her own across the table just in time to slide it deftly away from* Helen's *pouncing hand. She lifts the hand and moves it to* Helen's *plate, and after an instant's exploration,* Helen *sits again on the floor and drums her heels.* Annie *comes around the table and resumes her chair.*

When Helen *feels her skirt again, she ceases kicking, waits for whatever is to come, renews some kicking, waits again.* Annie *retrieving her plate takes up a forkful of food, stops it halfway to her mouth, gazes at it devoid of appetite, and half-lowers it; but after a look at* Helen *she sighs, dips the forkful toward* Helen *in a for-your-sake toast, and puts it in her own mouth to chew, not without an effort.*

Helen *now gets hold of the chair leg, and half-succeeds in pulling the chair out from under her.* Annie *bangs it down with her rear, heavily, and sits with all her weight.* Helen's *next attempt to topple it is unavailing, so her fingers dive in a pinch at* Annie's *flank.* Annie *in the middle of her mouthful almost loses it with startle, and she slaps down her fork to round on* Helen. *The child comes up with curiosity to feel what* Annie *is doing, so* Annie *resumes eating, letting* Helen's *hand follow the movement of her fork to her mouth; whereupon* Helen *at once reaches into* Annie's *plate.* Annie *firmly removes her hand to her own plate.* Helen *in reply pinches* Annie's *thigh, a good mean pinchful that makes* Annie *jump.* Annie *sets the fork down, and sits with her mouth tight.* Helen *digs another pinch into her thigh, and this time* Annie *slaps her hand smartly away;* Helen *retaliates with a roundhouse fist that catches* Annie *on the ear, and* Annie's *hand leaps at once in a forceful slap across* Helen's *cheek;* Helen *is the startled one now.* Annie's *hand in compunction falters to her own face, but when* Helen *hits at her again,* Annie *deliberately slaps her again.* Helen *lifts her fist irresolute for another roundhouse,* Annie *lifts her hand resolute for another slap, and they freeze in this posture, while* Helen *mulls it over. She thinks better of it, drops her fist, and giving* Annie *a wide berth, gropes around to her Mother's chair, to find it empty; she blunders her way along the table upstage, and encountering the empty chairs and missing plates, she looks bewildered; she gropes back to her Mother's chair, again touches her cheek and indicates the chair, and waits for the world to answer.*

Annie *now reaches over to spell into her hand, but* Helen *yanks it away; she gropes to the front door, tries the knob, and finds the door locked, with no key. She gropes to the rear door, and finds it locked, with no key. She commences to bang on it.* Annie *rises, crosses, takes her wrists, draws her resisting back to the table, seats her, and releases her hands upon her plate; as* Annie *herself begins to sit,* Helen *writhes out of her chair, runs to the front door, and tugs and kicks at it.* Annie *rises again, crosses, draws her by one wrist back to the table, seats her, and sits;* Helen *escapes back to the door, knocking over her Mother's chair en route.* Annie *rises again in pursuit, and this time lifts* Helen *bodily from behind and bears her kicking to her chair. She deposits her, and once more turns to sit.* Helen *scrambles out, but as she passes* Annie *catches her up again from behind and deposits her in the chair;* Helen *scrambles out on the other side, for the rear door, but* Annie *at her heels catches her up and deposits her again in the chair. She stands behind it.* Helen *scrambles out to her right, and the instant her feet hit the floor* Annie *lifts and deposits her back; she scrambles out to her left, and is at once lifted and deposited back. She tries right again and is deposited back, and tries left again and is deposited back, and now feints* Annie *to the right but is off to her left, and is promptly deposited back. She sits a moment, and then starts straight over the tabletop, dishware notwithstanding;* Annie *hauls her in and deposits her back, with her plate spilling in her lap, and she melts to the floor and crawls under the table, laborious among its legs and chairs; but* Annie *is swift around the table and waiting on the other side when she surfaces, immediately bearing her aloft;* Helen *clutches at* James's *chair for anchorage, but it comes with her, and halfway back she abandons it to the floor.* Annie *deposits her in her chair, and waits.* Helen *sits tensed motionless. Then she tentatively puts out her left foot and hand,* Annie *interposes her own hand, and at the contact* Helen *jerks hers in. She tries her right foot,* Annie *blocks it with her own, and* Helen *jerks hers in. Finally, leaning back, she slumps down in her chair, in a sullen biding.*

Annie *backs off a step, and watches;* Helen *offers no move.* Annie *takes a deep breath. Both of them and the room are in considerable disorder, two chairs down and the table a mess, but* Annie *makes no effort to tidy it; she only sits on her own chair, and lets her energy refill. Then she takes up knife and fork, and resolutely addresses her food.* Helen's *hand comes out to explore, and seeing it* Annie *sits without moving, the child's hand goes over her hand and fork, pauses—*Annie *still does not move—and withdraws. Presently it moves for her own plate, slaps about for it, and stops, thwarted. At this,* Annie *again rises, recovers* Helen's *plate from the floor and a handful of scattered food from the deranged tablecloth, drops it on the plate, and pushes the plate into contact with* Helen's *fist. Neither of them now moves for a pregnant moment—until* Helen *suddenly takes a grab of food and wolfs it down.* Annie *permits herself the humor of a minor bow and warming of her hands together; she wanders off a step or two, watching.* Helen *cleans up the plate.*

After a glower of indecision, she holds the empty plate out for more. Annie *accepts it, and crossing to the removed plates, spoons food from them onto it; she stands debating the spoon, tapping it a few times on* Helen's *plate; and when she returns with the plate she brings the spoon, too. She puts the spoon first into* Helen's *hand, then sets the plate down.* Helen *discarding the spoon reaches with her hand, and* Annie *stops it by the wrist; she replaces the spoon in it.* Helen *impatiently discards it again, and again* Annie *stops her hand, to replace the spoon in it. This time* Helen *throws the spoon on the floor.* Annie *after considering it lifts* Helen *bodily out of the chair, and in a wrestling match on the floor closes her fingers upon the spoon, and returns her with it to the chair.* Helen *again throws the spoon on the floor.* Annie *lifts her out of the chair again; but in the struggle over the spoon Helen with Annie on her back sends her sliding over her head; Helen flees back to her chair and scrambles into it. When Annie comes after her she clutches it for dear life; Annie pries one hand loose, then the other, then the first again, then the other again, and then lifts Helen by the waist, chair and all, and shakes the chair loose. Helen wrestles to get free, but Annie pins her to the floor, closes her fingers upon the spoon, and lifts her kicking under one arm; with her other hand she gets the chair in place again, and plunks Helen back on it. When she releases her hand, Helen throws the spoon at her.*

Annie now removes the plate of food. Helen grabbing finds it missing, and commences to bang with her fists on the table. Annie collects a fistful of spoons and descends with them and the plate on Helen; she lets her smell the plate, at which Helen ceases banging, and Annie puts the plate down and a spoon in Helen's hand. Helen throws it on the floor. Annie puts another spoon in her hand. Helen throws it on the floor. Annie puts another spoon in her hand. Helen throws it on the floor. When Annie comes to her last spoon she sits next to Helen, and gripping the spoon in Helen's hand compels her to take food in it up to her mouth. Helen sits with lips shut. Annie waits a stolid moment, then lowers Helen's hand. She tries again; Helen's lips remain shut. Annie waits, lowers Helen's hand. She tries again; this time Helen suddenly opens her mouth and accepts the food. Annie lowers the spoon with a sigh of relief, and Helen spews the mouthful out at her face. Annie sits a moment with eyes closed, then takes the pitcher and dashes its water into Helen's face, who gasps astonished. Annie with Helen's hand takes up another spoonful, and shoves it into her open mouth. Helen swallows involuntarily, and while she is catching her breath Annie forces her palm open, throws four swift letters into it, then another four, and bows toward her with devastating pleasantness.)

Annie. Good girl.

(Annie *lifts* Helen's *hand to feel her face nodding;* Helen *grabs a fistful of her hair, and yanks. The pain brings* Annie *to her knees, and* Helen *pummels her; they roll under the table, and the lights commence to dim out on them.*

Simultaneously the light at left has been rising, slowly, so slowly that it seems at first we only imagine what is intimated in the yard: a few ghostlike figures, in silence, motionless, waiting. Now the distant belfry chimes commence to toll the hour, also very slowly, almost—it is twelve—interminably; the sense is that of a long time passing. We can identify the figures before the twelfth stroke, all facing the house in a kind of watch: Kate *is standing exactly as before, but now with the baby* Mildred *sleeping in her arms, and placed here and there, unmoving, are* Aunt Ev *in her hat with a hanky to her nose, and the two Negro children,* Percy *and* Martha *with necks outstretched eagerly, and* Viney *with a knotted kerchief on her head and a feather duster in her hand.*

The chimes cease, and there is silence. For a long moment none of the group moves.)

Viney (*presently*). What am I gone do, Miss Kate? It's noontime, dinner's comin', I didn't get them breakfast dishes out of there yet.

(Kate *says nothing, stares at the house.* Martha *shifts* Helen's *doll in her clutch, and it plaintively says* momma.)

Kate (*presently*). You run along, Martha.

(Aunt Ev *blows her nose.*)

Aunt Ev (*wretchedly*). I can't wait out here a minute longer, Kate, why, this could go on all afternoon, too.

Kate. I'll tell the captain you called.

Viney (*to the children*). You hear what Miss Kate say? Never you mind what's going on here.

(*Still no one moves.*)

You run along tend your own bizness.

(*Finally* Viney *turns on the children with the feather duster.*)

Shoo!

(*The two children divide before her. She chases them off.* Aunt Ev *comes to* Kate, *on her dignity.*)

Aunt Ev. Say what you like, Kate, but that child is a *Keller.*

(*She opens her parasol, preparatory to leaving.*)

I needn't remind you that all the Kellers are cousins to General Robert E. Lee. I don't know *who* that girl is.

(*She waits; but* Kate *staring at the house is without response.*)

The only Sullivan I've heard of—from Boston too, and I'd think twice before locking her up with that kind—is that man John L.

(*And* Aunt Ev *departs, with head high. Presently* Viney *comes to* Kate, *her arms out for the baby.*)

Viney. You give me her, Miss Kate, I'll sneak her in back, to her crib.

(*But* Kate *is moveless, until* Viney *starts to take the baby;* Kate *looks down at her before relinquishing her.*)

Kate (*slowly*). This child never gives me a minute's worry.

Viney. Oh yes, this one's the angel of the family, no question bout *that.*

(*She begins off rear with the baby, heading around the house; and* Kate *now turns her back on it, her hand to her eyes. At this moment there is the slamming of a door, and when* Kate *wheels* Helen *is blundering down the porch steps into the light, like a ruined bat out of hell.* Viney *halts, and* Kate *runs in;* Helen *collides with her mother's knees, and reels off and back to clutch them as her savior.* Annie *with smoked glasses in hand stands on the porch, also much undone, looking as though she had indeed just taken Vicksburg.* Kate *taking in* Helen's *ravaged state becomes steely in her gaze up at* Annie.)

Kate. What happened?

(Annie *meets* Kate's *gaze, and gives a factual report, too exhausted for anything but a flat voice.*)

Annie. She ate from her own plate.

(*She thinks a moment.*)

She ate with a spoon. Herself.

(Kate *frowns, uncertain with thought, and glances down at* Helen.)

And she folded her napkin.

(Kate's *gaze now wavers, from* Helen *to* Annie, *and back.*)

Kate (*softly*). Folded—her napkin?

Annie. The room's a wreck, but her napkin is folded.

(*She pauses, then:*)

I'll be in my room, Mrs. Keller.

(*She moves to re-enter the house; but she stops at* Viney's *voice.*)

Viney (*cheery*). Don't be long, Miss Annie. Dinner be ready right away!

(Viney *carries* Mildred *around the back of the house.* Annie *stands unmoving, takes a deep breath, stares over her shoulder at* Kate *and* Helen, *then inclines her head graciously, and goes with a slight stagger into the house. The lights in her room above steal up in readiness for her.*

Kate *remains alone with* Helen *in the yard, standing protectively over her, in a kind of wonder.*)

Kate (*slowly*). Folded her napkin.

(*She contemplates the wild head in her thighs, and moves her fingertips over it, with such a tenderness, and something like a fear of its strangeness, that her own eyes close; she whispers, bending to it:*)

My Helen—folded her napkin—

(*And still erect, with only her head in surrender,* Kate *for the first time that we see loses her protracted war with grief; but she will not let a sound escape her, only the grimace of tears comes, and sobs that shake her in a grip of silence. But* Helen *feels them, and her hand comes up in its own wondering, to interrogate her mother's face, until* Kate *buries her lips in the child's palm.*

Upstairs, Annie *enters her room, closes the door, and stands back against it; the lights, growing on her with their special color, commence to fade on* Kate *and* Helen. *Then* Annie *goes wearily to her suitcase, and lifts it to take it toward the bed. But it knocks an object to the floor, and she turns back to regard it. A new voice comes in a cultured murmur, hesitant as with the effort of remembering a text:*)

Man's voice. This—soul—

(Annie *puts the suitcase down, and kneels to the object: it is the battered Perkins report, and she stands with it in her hand, letting memory try to speak:*)

This—blind, deaf, mute—woman—

(Annie *sits on her bed, opens the book, and finding the*

passage, brings it up an inch from her eyes to read, her face and lips following the overheard words, the voice quite factual now:)

Can nothing be done to disinter this human soul? The whole neighborhood would rush to save this woman if she were buried alive by the caving in of a pit, and labor with zeal until she were dug out. Now if there were one who had as much patience as zeal, he might awaken her to a consciousness of her immortal—

(When the boy's voice comes, Annie closes her eyes, in pain.)

Boy's voice. Annie? Annie, you there?

Annie. Hush.

Boy's voice. Annie, what's that noise?

(Annie tries not to answer; her own voice is drawn out of her, unwilling.)

Annie. Just a cot, Jimmie.

Boy's voice. Where they pushin' it?

Annie. To the deadhouse.

Boy's voice. Annie. Does it hurt, to be dead?

(Annie escapes by opening her eyes, her hand works restlessly over her cheek; she retreats into the book again, but the cracked old crones interrupt, whispering. Annie slowly lowers the book.)

First Crone's voice. There is schools.

Second Crone's voice. There is schools outside—

Third Crone's voice. —schools where they teach blind ones, worse'n you—

First Crone's voice. To read—

Second Crone's voice. To read and write—

Third Crone's voice. There is schools outside where they—

First Crone's voice. There is schools—

(*Silence. Annie sits with her eyes shining, her hand almost in a caress over the book. Then:*)

Boy's voice. You ain't goin' to school, are you, Annie?

Annie (*whispering*). When I grow up.

Boy's voice. You ain't either, Annie. You're goin' to stay here take care of me.

Annie. I'm goin' to school when I grow up.

Boy's voice. You said we'll be together, forever and ever and ever—

Annie (*fierce*). I'm goin' to school when I grow up!

Doctor's voice (*slowly*). Little girl. Little girl, I must tell you. Your brother will be going on a journey, soon.

(Annie *sits rigid, in silence. Then the boy's voice pierces it, a shriek of terror.*)

Boy's voice. *Annie!*

(*It goes into* Annie *like a sword, she doubles onto it; the book falls to the floor. It takes her a racked moment to find herself and what she was engaged in here; when she sees the suitcase she remembers, and lifts it once again toward the bed. But the voices are with her, as she halts with suitcase in hand.*)

First Crone's voice. Goodbye, Annie.

Doctor's voice. Write me when you learn how.

Second Crone's voice. Don't tell anyone you came from here. Don't tell anyone—

Third Crone's voice. Yeah, don't tell anyone you came from—

First Crone's voice. Yeah, don't tell anyone—

Second Crone's voice. Don't tell any—

(The echoing voices fade. After a moment Annie *lays the suitcase on the bed; and the last voice comes faintly, from far away.)*

Boy's voice. Annie. It hurts, to be dead. Forever.

*(*Annie *falls to her knees by the bed, stifling her mouth in it. When at last she rolls blindly away from it, her palm comes down on the open report; she opens her eyes, regards it dully, and then, still on her knees, takes in the print.)*

Man's voice *(factual).* —might awaken her to a consciousness of her immortal nature. The chance is small indeed; but with a smaller chance they would have dug desperately for her in the pit; and is the life of the soul of less import than that of the body?

*(*Annie *gets to her feet. She drops the book on the bed, and pauses over her suitcase; after a moment she unclasps and opens it. Standing before it, she comes to her decision; she at once turns to the bureau, and taking her things out of its drawers, commences to throw them into the open suitcase.*

In the darkness down left a hand strikes a match, and lights a hanging oil lamp. It is Keller's *hand, and his voice accompanies it, very angry; the lights rising here before they fade on* Annie *show* Keller *and* Kate *inside a suggestion of a garden house, with a bay-window seat towards center and a door at back.)*

Keller. Katie, I will not *have* it! Now you did not see when that girl after supper tonight went to look for Helen in her room—

Kate. No.

Keller. The child practically climbed out of her window to escape from her! What kind of teacher *is* she? I thought I had seen her at her worst this morning, shouting at me, but I come home to find the entire house disorganized by her—Helen won't stay one second in the same room, won't come to the table with her, won't let herself be bathed or undressed or put to bed by her, or even by Viney now, and the end result is that *you* have to do more for the child than before we hired this girl's services! From the moment she stepped off the train she's been nothing but a burden, incompetent, impertinent, ineffectual, immodest—

Kate. She folded her napkin, Captain.

Keller. What?

Kate. Not ineffectual. Helen did fold her napkin.

Keller. What in heaven's name is so extraordinary about folding a napkin?

Kate (*with some humor*). Well. It's more than you did, Captain.

Keller. Katie. I did not bring you all the way out here to the garden house to be frivolous. Now, how does Miss Sullivan propose to teach a deaf-blind pupil who won't let her even touch her?

Kate (*a pause*). I don't know.

Keller. The fact is, today she scuttled any chance she ever had of getting along with the child. If you can see any point or purpose to her staying on here longer, it's more than—

Kate. What do you wish me to do?

Keller. I want you to give her notice.

Kate. I can't.

Keller. Then if you won't, I must. I simply will not—

(*He is interrupted by a knock at the back door.* Keller *after a glance at* Kate *moves to open the door;* Annie *in her smoked glasses is standing outside.* Keller *contemplates her, heavily.*)

Miss Sullivan.

Annie. Captain Keller.

(*She is nervous, keyed up to seizing the bull by the horns again, and she assumes a cheeriness which is not unshaky.*)

Viney said I'd find you both over here in the garden house. I thought we should—have a talk?

Keller (*reluctantly*). Yes, I— Well, come in.

(Annie *enters, and is interested in this room; she rounds on her heel, anxiously, studying it.* Keller *turns the matter over to* Kate, *sotto voce.*)

Katie.

Kate (*turning it back, courteously*). Captain.

(Keller *clears his throat, makes ready.*)

Keller. I, ah—wanted first to make my position clear to Mrs. Keller, in private. I have decided I—am not satisfied—in fact, am deeply dissatisfied—with the manner in which—

Annie (*intent*). Excuse me, is this little house ever in use?

Keller (*with patience*). In the hunting season. If you will give me your attention, Miss Sullivan.

(Annie *turns her smoked glasses upon him; they hold his unwilling stare.*)

I have tried to make allowances for you because you come from a part of the country where people are—women, I should say—come from who—well, for whom—

(*It begins to elude him.*)

—allowances must—be made. I have decided, nevertheless, to—that is, decided I—

(*Vexedly*)

Miss Sullivan, I find it difficult to talk through those glasses.

Annie (*eagerly, removing them*). Oh, of course.

Keller (*dourly*). Why do you wear them, the sun has been down for an hour.

Annie (*pleasantly, at the lamp*). Any kind of light hurts my eyes.

(*A silence;* Keller *ponders her, heavily.*)

Keller. Put them on. Miss Sullivan, I have decided to—give you another chance.

Annie (*cheerfully*). To do what?

Keller. To—remain in our employ.

(Annie's *eyes widen.*)

But on two conditions. I am not accustomed to rudeness in servants or women, and that is the first. If you are to stay, there must be a radical change of manner.

Annie (*a pause*). Whose?

Keller (*exploding*). Yours, young lady, isn't it obvious?

And the second is that you persuade me there's the slightest hope of your teaching a child who flees from you now like the plague, to anyone else she can find in this house.

Annie (*a pause*). There isn't.

(Kate *stops sewing, and fixes her eyes upon* Annie.)

Kate. What, Miss Annie?

Annie. It's hopeless here. I can't teach a child who runs away.

Keller (*nonplussed*). Then—do I understand you—propose—

Annie. Well, if we all agree it's hopeless, the next question is what—

Kate. Miss Annie.

(*She is leaning toward* Annie, *in deadly earnest; it commands both* Annie *and* Keller.)

I am not agreed. I think perhaps you—underestimate Helen.

Annie. I think everybody else here does.

Kate. She did fold her napkin. She learns, she learns, do you know she began talking when she was six months old? She could say "water." Not really—"wahwah." "Wahwah," but she meant water, she knew what it meant, and only six months old, I never saw a child so—bright, or outgoing—

(*Her voice is unsteady, but she gets it level.*)

It's still in her, somewhere, isn't it? You should have seen her before her illness, such a good-tempered child—

Annie (*agreeably*). She's changed.

(*A pause,* Kate *not letting her eyes go; her appeal at last is unconditional, and very quiet.*)

Kate. Miss Annie, put up with it. And with us.

Keller. Us!

Kate. Please? Like the lost lamb in the parable, I love her all the more.

Annie. Mrs. Keller, I don't think Helen's worst handicap is deafness or blindness. I think it's your love. And pity.

Keller. Now what does that mean?

Annie. All of you here are so sorry for her you've kept her—like a pet, why, even a dog you housebreak. No wonder she won't let me come near her. It's useless for me to try to teach her language or anything else here. I might as well—

Kate (*cuts in*). Miss Annie, before you came we spoke of putting her in an asylum.

(Annie *turns back to regard her. A pause.*)

Annie. What kind of asylum?

Keller. For mental defectives.

Kate. I visited there. I can't tell you what I saw, people like—animals, with—*rats*, in the halls, and—

(*She shakes her head on her vision.*)

What else are we to do, if you give up?

Annie. Give up?

Kate. You said it was hopeless.

Annie. Here. Give up, why, I only today saw what has to be done, to begin!

(*She glances from* Kate *to* Keller, *who stare, waiting; and she makes it as plain and simple as her nervousness permits.*)

I—want complete charge of her.

Keller. You already have that. It has resulted in—

Annie. No, I mean day and night. She has to be dependent on me.

Kate. For what?

Annie. Everything. The food she eats, the clothes she wears, fresh—

(*She is amused at herself, though very serious.*)

—air, yes, the air she breathes, whatever her body needs is a—primer, to teach her out of. It's the only way, the one who lets her have it should be her teacher.

(*She considers them in turn; they digest it,* Keller *frowning,* Kate *perplexed.*)

Not anyone who *loves* her, you have so many feelings they fall over each other like feet, you won't use your chances and you won't let me.

Kate. But if she runs from you—*to* us—

Annie. Yes, that's the point. I'll have to live with her somewhere else.

Keller. What!

Annie. Till she learns to depend on and listen to me.

Kate (*not without alarm*). For how long?

Annie. As long as it takes.

(*A pause. She takes a breath.*)

I packed half my things already.

Keller. Miss—Sullivan!

(*But when* Annie *attends upon him he is speechless, and she is merely earnest.*)

Annie. Captain Keller, it meets both your conditions. It's the one way I can get back in touch with Helen, and I don't see how I can be rude to you again if you're not around to interfere with me.

Keller (*red-faced*). And what is your intention if I say no? Pack the other half, for home, and abandon your charge to—to—

Annie. The asylum?

(*She waits, appraises* Keller's *glare and* Kate's *uncertainty, and decides to use her weapons.*)

I grew up in such an asylum. The state almshouse.

(Kate's *head comes up on this, and* Keller *stares hard;* Annie's *tone is cheerful enough, albeit level as gunfire.*)

Rats—why, my brother Jimmie and I used to play with the rats because we didn't have toys. Maybe you'd like to know what Helen will find there, not on visiting days? One ward was full of the—old women, crippled, blind, most of them dying, but even if what they had was catching there was nowhere else to move them, and that's where they put us. There were younger ones across the hall, prostitutes mostly, with T.B., and epileptic fits, and a couple of the kind who—keep after other girls, especially young ones, and some insane. Some just had the D.T.'s. The youngest were in another ward to have babies they didn't want, they started at thirteen, fourteen. They'd leave afterwards, but the babies stayed and we played with them, too, though a lot of them had—sores all over from diseases you're not supposed to talk about, but not many of them lived. The first year we had eighty, seventy died. The room Jimmie and I played in was the deadhouse, where they kept the bodies till they could dig—

Kate (*closes her eyes*). Oh, my dear—

Annie. —the graves.

(*She is immune to Kate's compassion.*)

No, it made me strong. But I don't think you need send Helen there. She's strong enough.

(*She waits again; but when neither offers her a word, she simply concludes.*)

No, I have no conditions, Captain Keller.

Kate (*not looking up*). Miss Annie.

Annie. Yes.

Kate (*a pause*). Where would you—take Helen?

Annie. Ohh—

(*Brightly*)

Italy?

Keller (*wheeling*). What?

Annie. Can't have everything, how would this garden house do? Furnish it, bring Helen here after a long ride so she won't recognize it, and you can see her every day. If she doesn't know. Well?

Kate (*a sigh of relief*). Is that all?

Annie. That's all.

Kate. Captain.

(*Keller turns his head; and Kate's request is quiet but firm.*)

With your permission?

Keller (*teeth in cigar*). Why must she depend on you for the food she eats?

Annie (*a pause*). I want control of it.

Keller. Why?

Annie. It's a way to reach her.

Keller (*stares*). You intend to *starve* her into letting you touch her?

Annie. She won't starve, she'll learn. All's fair in love and war, Captain Keller, you never cut supplies?

Keller. This is hardly a war!

Annie. Well, it's not love. A siege is a siege.

Keller (*heavily*). Miss Sullivan. Do you *like* the child?

Annie (*straight in his eyes*). Do you?

(*A long pause.*)

Kate. You could have a servant here—

Annie (*amused*). I'll have enough work without looking after a servant! But that boy Percy could sleep here, run errands—

Kate (*also amused*). We can let Percy sleep here, I think, Captain?

Annie (*eagerly*). And some old furniture, all our own—

Kate (*also eager*). Captain? Do you think that walnut bedstead in the barn would be too—

Keller. I have not yet consented to Percy! Or to the house, or to the proposal! Or to Miss Sullivan's— staying on when I—

(*But he erupts in an irate surrender.*)

Very well, I consent to everything!

(*He shakes the cigar at* Annie.)

For two weeks. I'll give you two weeks in this place, and it will be a miracle if you get the child to tolerate you.

Kate. Two weeks? Miss Annie, can you accomplish anything in two weeks?

Keller. Anything or not, two weeks, then the child comes back to us. Make up your mind, Miss Sullivan, yes or no?

Annie. Two weeks. For only one miracle?

(*She nods at him, nervously.*)

I'll get her to tolerate me.

(Keller *marches out, and slams the door.* Kate *on her feet regards* Annie, *who is facing the door.*)

Kate (*then*). You can't think as little of love as you said.

(Annie *glances questioning.*)

Or you wouldn't stay.

Annie (*a pause*). I didn't come here for love. I came for money!

(Kate *shakes her head to this, with a smile; after a moment she extends her open hand.* Annie *looks at it, but when she puts hers out it is not to shake hands, it is to set her fist in* Kate's *palm.*)

Kate (*puzzled*). Hm?

Annie. A. It's the first of many. Twenty-six!

(Kate *squeezes her fist, squeezes it hard, and hastens out after* Keller. Annie *stands as the door closes behind her, her manner so apprehensive that finally she slaps her brow, holds it, sighs, and, with her eyes closed, crosses herself for luck.*

The lights dim into a cool silhouette scene around her, the lamp paling out, and now, in formal entrances, persons appear around Annie *with furniture for the room:* Percy *crosses the stage with a rocking chair and waits;* Martha *from another direction bears in a stool,* Viney *bears in a small table, and the other Negro servant rolls in a bed part-way from left; and* Annie, *opening her eyes to put her glasses back on, sees them. She turns around in the room once, and goes into action, pointing out locations for each article; the servants place them and leave, and* Annie *then darts around, interchanging them. In the midst of this—while* Percy *and* Martha *reappear with a tray of food and a chair, respectively—*James *comes down from the house with* Annie's *suitcase, and stands viewing the room and her quizzically;* Annie *halts abruptly under his eyes, embarrassed, then seizes the suitcase from his hand, explaining herself brightly.)*

Annie. I always wanted to live in a doll's house!

(She sets the suitcase out of the way, and continues; Viney *at left appears to position a rod with drapes for a doorway, and the other servant at center pushes in a wheelbarrow loaded with a couple of boxes of* Helen's *toys and clothes.* Annie *helps lift them into the room, and the servant pushes the wheelbarrow off. In none of this is any heed taken of the imaginary walls of the garden house, the furniture is moved in from every side and itself defines the walls.*

Annie *now drags the box of toys into center, props up the doll conspicuously on top; with the people melted away, except for* James, *all is again still. The lights turn again without pause, rising warmer.)*

James. You don't let go of things easily, do you? How will you—win her hand now, in this place?

Annie (*curtly*). Do I know? I lost my temper, and here we are!

James (*lightly*). No touching, no teaching. Of course, you *are* bigger—

Annie. I'm not counting on force, I'm counting on her. That little imp is dying to know.

James. Know what?

Annie. Anything. Any and every crumb in God's creation. I'll have to use that appetite too.

(*She gives the room a final survey, straightens the bed, arranges the curtains.*)

James (*a pause*). Maybe she'll teach you.

Annie. Of course.

James. That she isn't. That there's such a thing as—dullness of heart. Acceptance. And letting go. Sooner or later we all give up, don't we?

Annie. Maybe you all do. It's my idea of the original sin.

James. What is?

Annie (*witheringly*). Giving up.

James (*nettled*). You won't open her. Why can't you let her be? Have some—pity on her, for being what she is—

Annie. If I'd ever once thought like that, I'd be dead!

James (*pleasantly*). You will be. Why trouble?

(Annie *turns to glare at him; he is mocking.*)

Or will you teach me?

(*And with a bow, he drifts off.*

Now in the distance there comes the clopping of hoofs, drawing near, and nearer, up to the door; and they halt. Annie wheels to face the door. *When it opens this time, the* Kellers—Kate *in travelling bonnet,* Keller *also hatted—are standing there with* Helen *between them; she is in a cloak.* Kate *gently cues her into the room.* Helen *comes in groping, baffled, but interested in the new surroundings;* Annie *evades her exploring hand, her gaze not leaving the child.*)

Annie. Does she know where she is?

Kate (*shakes her head*). We rode her out in the country for two hours.

Keller. For all she knows, she could be in another town—

(Helen *stumbles over the box on the floor and in it discovers her doll and other battered toys, is pleased, sits to them, then becomes puzzled and suddenly very wary. She scrambles up and back to her mother's thighs, but* Annie *steps in, and it is hers that* Helen *embraces.* Helen *recoils, gropes, and touches her cheek instantly.*)

Kate. That's her sign for me.

Annie. I know.

(Helen *waits, then recommences her groping, more urgently.* Kate *stands indecisive, and takes an abrupt step toward her, but* Annie's *hand is a barrier.*)

In two weeks.

Kate. Miss Annie, I— Please be good to her. These two weeks, try to be very good to her—

Annie. I will.

(Kate, *turning then, hurries out. The* Kellers *cross back of the main house.*

Annie *closes the door.* Helen *starts at the door jar, and rushes it.* Annie *holds her off.* Helen *kicks her, breaks free, and careens around the room like an imprisoned bird, colliding with furniture, groping wildly, repeatedly touching her cheek in a growing panic. When she has covered the room, she commences her weird screaming.* Annie *moves to comfort her, but her touch sends* Helen *into a paroxysm of rage: she tears away, falls over her box of toys, flings its contents in handfuls in* Annie's *direction, flings the box too, reels to her feet, rips curtains from the window, bangs and kicks at the door, sweeps objects off the mantelpiece and shelf, a little tornado incarnate, all destruction, until she comes upon her doll and, in the act of hurling it, freezes. Then she clutches it to herself, and in exhaustion sinks sobbing to the floor.* Annie *stands contemplating her, in some awe.*)

Two weeks.

(*She shakes her head, not without a touch of disgusted bewilderment.*)

What did I get into now?

(*The lights have been dimming throughout, and the garden house is lit only by moonlight now, with* Annie *lost in the patches of dark.*

Kate, *now hatless and coatless, enters the family room by the rear door, carrying a lamp.* Keller, *also hatless, wanders simultaneously around the back of the main house to where* James *has been waiting, in the rising moonlight, on the porch.*)

Keller. I can't understand it. I had every intention of dismissing that girl, not setting her up like an empress.

James. Yes, what's her secret, sir?

Keller. Secret?

James (*pleasantly*). That enables her to get anything she wants out of you? When I can't.

(James *turns to go into the house, but* Keller *grasps his wrist, twisting him half to his knees.* Kate *comes from the porch.*)

Keller (*angrily*). She does *not* get anything she—

James (*in pain*). Don't—don't—

Kate. Captain.

Keller. He's afraid.

(*He throws* James *away from him, with contempt.*)

What *does* he want out of me?

James (*an outcry*). My God, don't you know?

(*He gazes from* Keller *to* Kate.)

Everything you forgot, when you forgot my mother.

Keller. What!

(James *wheels into the house.* Keller *takes a stride to the porch, to roar after him.*)

One thing that girl's secret is not, she doesn't fire one shot and disappear!

(Kate *stands rigid, and* Keller *comes back to her.*)

Katie. Don't mind what he—

Kate. Captain, *I* am proud of you.

Keller. For what?

Kate. For letting this girl have what she needs.

Keller. Why can't my son be? He can't bear me, you'd

think I treat him as hard as this girl does Helen—

(*He breaks off, as it dawns in him.*)

Kate (*gently*). Perhaps you do.

Keller. But he has to learn some respect!

Kate (*a pause, wryly*). *Do* you like the child?

(*She turns again to the porch, but pauses, reluctant.*)

How empty the house is, tonight.

(*After a moment she continues on in.* Keller *stands move-less, as the moonlight dies on him.*

The distant belfry chimes toll, two o'clock, and with them, a moment later, comes the boy's voice on the wind, in a whisper:)

Boy's voice. Annie. Annie.

(*In her patch of dark* Annie, *now in her nightgown, hurls a cup into a corner as though it were her grief, getting rid of its taste through her teeth.*)

Annie. No! No pity, I won't have it.

(*She comes to* Helen, *prone on the floor.*)

On either of us.

(*She goes to her knees, but when she touches* Helen's *hand the child starts up awake, recoils, and scrambles away from her under the bed.* Annie *stares after her. She strikes her palm on the floor, with passion.*)

I *will* touch you!

(*She gets to her feet, and paces in a kind of anger around the bed, her hand in her hair, and confronting* Helen *at each turn.*)

How, how? How do I—

(Annie *stops. Then she calls out urgently, loudly.*)

Percy! Percy!

(*She moves swiftly to the drapes, at left.*)

Percy, wake up!

(*Percy's voice comes in a thick sleepy mumble, unintelligible.*)

Get out of bed and come in here, I need you.

(Annie *darts away, finds and strikes a match, and touches it to the hanging lamp; the lights come up dimly in the room, and* Percy *stands bare to the waist in torn overalls between the drapes, with eyes closed, swaying.* Annie *goes to him, pats his cheeks vigorously.*)

Percy. You awake?

Percy. No'm.

Annie. How would you like to play a nice game?

Percy. Whah?

Annie. With Helen. She's under the bed. Touch her hand.

(*She kneels* Percy *down at the bed, thrusting his hand under it to contact* Helen's; Helen *emits an animal sound and crawls to the opposite side, but commences sniffing.* Annie *rounds the bed with* Percy *and thrusts his hand again at* Helen; *this time* Helen *clutches it, sniffs in recognition, and comes scrambling out after* Percy, *to hug him with delight.* Percy *alarmed struggles, and* Helen's *fingers go to his mouth.*)

Percy. Lemme go. Lemme go—

(Helen *fingers her own lips, as before, moving them in dumb imitation.*)

She tryin' talk. She gonna hit me—

Annie (*grimly*). She *can* talk. If she only knew, I'll show you how. She makes letters.

(*She opens* Percy's *other hand, and spells into it:*)

This one is C. C.

(*She hits his palm with it a couple of times, her eyes upon* Helen *across him;* Helen *gropes to feel what* Percy's *hand is doing, and when she encounters* Annie's *she falls back from them.*)

She's mad at me now, though, she won't play. But she knows lots of letters. Here's another, A. C, a. C, a.

(*But she is watching* Helen, *who comes groping, consumed with curiosity;* Annie *makes the letters in* Percy's *hand, and* Helen *pokes to question what they are up to. Then* Helen *snatches* Percy's *other hand, and quickly spells four letters into it.* Annie *follows them aloud.*)

C, a, k, e! She spells cake, she gets cake.

(*She is swiftly over to the tray of food, to fetch cake and a jug of milk.*)

She doesn't know yet it means this. Isn't it funny she knows how to spell it and doesn't *know* she knows?

(*She breaks the cake in two pieces, and extends one to each;* Helen *rolls away from her offer.*)

Well, if she won't play it with me, I'll play it with you. Would you like to learn one she doesn't know?

Percy. No'm.

(*But* Annie *seizes his wrist, and spells to him.*)

Annie. M, i, l, k. M is this. I, that's an easy one, just the little finger. L is this—

(*And* Helen *comes back with her hand, to feel the new word.* Annie *brushes her away, and continues spelling aloud to* Percy. Helen's *hand comes back again, and tries to get in;* Annie *brushes it away again.* Helen's *hand insists, and* Annie *puts it away rudely.*)

No, why should I talk to you? I'm teaching Percy a new word. L. K is this—

(Helen *now yanks their hands apart; she butts* Percy *away, and thrusts her palm out insistently.* Annie's *eyes are bright, with glee.*)

Ho, you're *jealous*, are you!

(Helen's *hand waits, intractably waits.*)

All *right*.

(Annie *spells into it, milk; and* Helen *after a moment spells it back to* Annie. Annie *takes her hand, with her whole face shining. She gives a great sigh.*)

Good! So I'm finally back to where I can touch you, hm? Touch and go! No love lost, but here we go.

(*She puts the jug of milk into* Helen's *hand and squeezes* Percy's *shoulder.*)

You can go to bed now, you've earned your sleep. Thank you.

(Percy *stumbling up weaves his way out through the drapes.* Helen *finishes drinking, and holds the jug out, for* Annie; *when* Annie *takes it,* Helen *crawls onto the bed, and makes for sleep.* Annie *stands, looks down at her.*)

Now all I have to teach you is—one word. Everything.

(*She sets the jug down. On the floor now* Annie *spies the doll, stoops to pick it up, and with it dangling in her hand, turns off the lamp. A shaft of moonlight is left on* Helen *in the bed, and a second shaft on the rocking chair; and* Annie, *after putting off her smoked glasses, sits in the rocker with the doll. She is rather happy, and dangles the doll on her knee, and it makes its momma sound.* Annie *whispers to it in mock solicitude.*)

Hush, little baby. Don't—say a word—

(*She lays it against her shoulder, and begins rocking with it, patting its diminutive behind; she talks the lullaby to it, humorously at first.*)

Momma's gonna buy you—a mockingbird:
If that—mockingbird don't sing—

(*The rhythm of the rocking takes her into the tune, softly, and more tenderly.*)

Momma's gonna buy you a diamond ring:
If that diamond ring turns to brass—

(*A third shaft of moonlight outside now rises to pick out* James *at the main house, with one foot on the porch step; he turns his body, as if hearing the song.*)

Momma's gonna buy you a looking-glass:
If that looking-glass gets broke—

(*In the family room a fourth shaft picks out* Keller *seated at the table, in thought; and he, too, lifts his head, as if hearing.*)

Momma's gonna buy you a billy goat:
If that billy goat won't pull—

(*The fifth shaft is upstairs in Annie's room, and picks out* Kate, *pacing there; and she halts, turning her head, too, as if hearing.*)

Momma's gonna buy you a cart and bull:
If that cart and bull turns over,

Momma's gonna buy you a dog named Rover;
If that dog named Rover won't bark—

(*With the shafts of moonlight on* Helen, *and* James, *and*
Keller, *and* Kate, *all moveless, and* Annie *rocking the doll,
the curtain ends the act.*)

.

ACT THREE

The stage is totally dark, until we see Annie *and* Helen *silhouetted on the bed in the garden house.* Annie's *voice is audible, very patient, and worn; it has been saying this for a long time.*

Annie. Water, Helen. This is water. W, a, t, e, r. It has a *name.*

(*A silence. Then:*)

Egg, e, g, g. It has a *name,* the name stands for the thing. Oh, it's so simple, simple as birth, to explain.

(*The lights have commenced to rise, not on the garden house but on the homestead. Then:*)

Helen, Helen, the chick *has* to come out of its shell, sometime. You come out, too.

(*In the bedroom upstairs, we see* Viney *unhurriedly washing the window, dusting, turning the mattress, readying the room for use again; then in the family room a diminished group at one end of the table—*Kate, Keller, James*—finishing up a quiet breakfast; then outside, down right, the other Negro servant on his knees, assisted by* Martha, *working with a trowel around a new trellis and wheelbarrow. The scene is one of everyday calm, and all are oblivious to* Annie's *voice.*)

There's only one way out, for you, and it's language. To learn that your fingers can talk. And say anything, anything you can name. This is mug.

Mug, m, u, g. Helen, it has a *name*. It—has—a—
name—

(Kate *rises from the table*.)

Keller (*gently*). You haven't eaten, Katie.

Kate (*smiles, shakes her head*). I haven't the appetite. I'm
too—restless, I can't sit to it.

Keller. You should eat, my dear. It will be a long day,
waiting.

James (*lightly*). But it's been a short two weeks. I never
thought life could be so—noiseless, went much too
quickly for me.

(Kate *and* Keller *gaze at him, in silence.* James *becomes
uncomfortable.*)

Annie. C, a, r, d. Card. C, a—

James. Well, the house has been practically normal,
hasn't it?

Keller (*harshly*). Jimmie.

James. Is it wrong to enjoy a quiet breakfast, after five
years? And you two even seem to enjoy each
other—

Keller. It could be even more noiseless, Jimmie,
without your tongue running every minute. Haven't
you enough feeling to imagine what Katie has been
undergoing, ever since—

(Kate *stops him, with her hand on his arm*.)

Kate. Captain.

(*To* James.)

It's true. The two weeks have been normal, quiet,
all you say. But not short. Interminable.

(*She rises, and wanders out; she pauses on the porch steps, gazing toward the garden house.*)

Annie (*fading*). W, a, t, e, r. But it means *this*. W, a, t, e, r. *This*. W, a, t—

James. I only meant that Miss Sullivan is a boon. Of contention, though, it seems.

Keller (*heavily*). If and when you're a parent, Jimmie, you will understand what separation means. A mother loses a—protector.

James (*baffled*). Hm?

Keller. You'll learn, we don't just keep our children safe. They keep us safe.

(*He rises, with his empty coffee cup and saucer.*)

There are of course all kinds of separation, Katie has lived with one kind for five years. And another is disappointment. In a child.

(*He goes with the cup out the rear door. James sits for a long moment of stillness. In the garden house the lights commence to come up; Annie, haggard at the table, is writing a letter, her face again almost in contact with the stationery; Helen, apart on the stool, and for the first time as clean and neat as a button, is quietly crocheting an endless chain of wool, which snakes all around the room.*)

Annie. "I, feel, every, day, more, and, more, in—"

(*She pauses, and turns the pages of a dictionary open before her; her finger descends the words to a full stop. She elevates her eyebrows, then copies the word.*)

"—adequate."

(*In the main house James pushes up, and goes to the front doorway, after Kate.*)

James. Kate?

(Kate *turns her glance.* James *is rather weary.*)

I'm sorry. Open my mouth, like that fairy tale, frogs jump out.

Kate. No. It has been better. For everyone.

(*She starts away, up center.*)

Annie (*writing*). "If, only, there, were, someone, to, help, me, I, need, a, teacher, as, much, as, Helen—"

James. Kate.

(Kate *halts, waits.*)

What does he want from me?

Kate. That's not the question. Stand up to the world, Jimmie, that comes first.

James (*a pause, wryly*). But the world is him.

Kate. Yes. And no one can do it for you.

James. Kate.

(*His voice is humble.*)

At least we— Could you—be my friend?

Kate. I am.

(Kate *turns to wander, up back of the garden house.* Annie's *murmur comes at once; the lights begin to die on the main house.*)

Annie. "—my, mind, is, undisiplined, full, of, skips, and, jumps, and—"

(*She halts, rereads, frowns.*)

Hm.

(Annie *puts her nose again in the dictionary, flips back to an earlier page, and fingers down the words;* Kate *presently comes down toward the bay window with a trayful of food.*)

Disinter—disinterested—disjoin—dis—

(*She backtracks, indignant.*)

Disinterested, disjoin— Where's disipline?

(*She goes a page or two back, searching with her finger, muttering.*)

What a dictionary, have to know how to spell it before you can look up how to spell it, disciple, *discipline!* Diskipline.

(*She corrects the word in her letter.*)

Undisciplined.

(*But her eyes are bothering her, she closes them in exhaustion and gently fingers the eyelids.* Kate *watches her through the window.*)

Kate. What are you doing to your eyes?

(Annie *glances around; she puts her smoked glasses on, and gets up to come over, assuming a cheerful energy.*)

Annie. It's worse on my vanity! I'm learning to spell. It's like a surprise party, the most unexpected characters turn up.

Kate. You're not to overwork your eyes, Miss Annie.

Annie. Well.

(*She takes the tray, sets it on her chair, and carries chair and tray to* Helen.)

Whatever I spell to Helen I'd better spell right.

Kate (*almost wistful*). How—serene she is.

Annie. She learned this stitch yesterday. Now I can't get her to stop!

(*She disentangles one foot from the wool chain, and sets the chair before* Helen. Helen *at its contact with her knee feels the plate, promptly sets her crocheting down, and tucks the napkin in at her neck, but* Annie *withholds the spoon; when* Helen *finds it missing, she folds her hands in her lap, and quietly waits.* Annie *twinkles at* Kate *with mock devoutness.*)

Such a little lady, she'd sooner starve than eat with her fingers.

(*She gives* Helen *the spoon, and* Helen *begins to eat, neatly.*)

Kate. You've taught her so much, these two weeks. I would never have—

Annie. Not enough.

(*She is suddenly gloomy, shakes her head.*)

Obedience isn't enough. Well, she learned two nouns this morning, key and water, brings her up to eighteen nouns and three verbs.

Kate (*hesitant*). But—not—

Annie. No. Not that they mean things. It's still a finger-game, no meaning.

(*She turns to* Kate, *abruptly.*)

Mrs. Keller—

(*But she defers it; she comes back, to sit in the bay and lift her hand.*)

Shall we play our finger-game?

Kate. How will she learn it?

Annie. It will come.

(*She spells a word; Kate does not respond.*)

Kate. How?

Annie (*a pause*). How does a bird learn to fly?

(*She spells again.*)

We're born to use words, like wings, it has to come.

Kate. How?

Annie (*another pause, wearily*). All right. I don't know how.

(*She pushes up her glasses, to rub her eyes.*)

I've done everything I could think of. Whatever she's learned here—keeping herself clean, knitting, stringing beads, meals, setting-up exercises each morning, we climb trees, hunt eggs, yesterday a chick was born in her hands—all of it I spell, everything we do, we never stop spelling. I go to bed with—writer's cramp from talking so much!

Kate. I worry about you, Miss Annie. You must rest.

Annie. Now? She spells back in her *sleep*, her fingers make letters when she doesn't know! In her bones those five fingers know, that hand aches to—speak out, and something in her mind is asleep, how do I—nudge that awake? That's the one question.

Kate. With no answer.

Annie (*long pause*). Except keep at it. Like this.

(*She again begins spelling—I, need—and* Kate's *brows gather, following the words.*)

Kate. More—time?

(*She glances at* Annie, *who looks her in the eyes, silent.*)

Here?

Annie. Spell it.

(Kate *spells a word—no—shaking her head;* Annie *spells two words—why, not—back, with an impatient question in her eyes; and* Kate *moves her head in pain to answer it.*)

Kate. Because I can't—

Annie. Spell it! If she ever learns, you'll have a lot to tell each other, start now.

(Kate *painstakingly spells in air. In the midst of this the rear door opens, and* Keller *enters with the setter* Belle *in tow.*)

Keller. Miss Sullivan? On my way to the office, I brought Helen a playmate—

Annie. Outside please, Captain Keller.

Keller. My dear child, the two weeks are up today, surely you don't object to—

Annie (*rising*). They're not up till six o'clock.

Keller (*indulgent*). Oh, now. What difference can a fraction of one day—

Annie. An agreement is an agreement. Now you've been very good, I'm sure you can keep it up for a few more hours.

(*She escorts* Keller *by the arm over the threshold; he obeys, leaving* Belle.)

Keller. Miss Sullivan, you are a tyrant.

Annie. Likewise, I'm sure. You can stand there, and close the door if she comes.

Kate. I don't think you know how eager we are to have her back in our arms—

Annie. I do know, it's my main worry.

Keller. It's like expecting a new child in the house.

Well, she *is*, so—composed, so—

(*Gently*)

Attractive. You've done wonders for her, Miss Sullivan.

Annie (*not a question*). Have I.

Keller. If there's anything you want from us in repayment tell us, it will be a privilege to—

Annie. I just told Mrs. Keller. I want more time.

Kate. Miss Annie—

Annie. Another week.

(Helen *lifts her head, and begins to sniff.*)

Keller. We miss the child. *I* miss her, I'm glad to say, that's a different debt I owe you—

Annie. Pay it to Helen. Give *her* another week.

Kate (*gently*). Doesn't she miss us?

Keller. Of course she does. What a wrench this unexplainable—exile must be to her, can you say it's not?

Annie. No. But I—

(Helen *is off the stool, to grope about the room; when she encounters* Belle, *she throws her arms around the dog's neck in delight.*)

Kate. Doesn't she need affection too, Miss Annie?

Annie (*wavering*). She—never shows me she needs it, she won't have any—caressing or—

Kate. But you're not her mother.

Keller. And what would another week accomplish? We are more than satisfied, you've done more than we ever thought possible, taught her constructive—

Annie. I can't promise anything. All I can—

Keller (*no break*). —things to do, to behave like—even look like—a human child, so manageable, contented, cleaner, more—

Annie (*withering*). Cleaner.

Keller. Well. We say cleanliness is next to godliness, Miss—

Annie. Cleanliness is next to nothing, she has to learn that everything has its name! That words can be her *eyes,* to everything in the world outside her, and inside too, what is she without words? With them she can think, have ideas, be reached, there's not a thought or fact in the world that can't be hers. You publish a newspaper, Captain Keller, do I have to tell you what words are? And she has them already—

Keller. Miss Sullivan.

Annie. —eighteen nouns and three verbs, they're in her fingers now, I need only time to push *one* of them into her mind! One, and everything under the sun will follow. Don't you see what she's learned here is only clearing the way for that? I can't risk her unlearning it, give me more time alone with her, another week to—

Keller. Look.

(*He* points, *and* Annie *turns.* Helen *is playing with* Belle's *claws; she makes letters with her fingers, shows them to* Belle, *waits with her palm, then manipulates the dog's claws.*)

What is she spelling?

(*A silence.*)

Kate. Water?

(Annie *nods.*)

Keller. Teaching a dog to spell.

(*A pause.*)

The dog doesn't know what she means, any more than she knows what you mean, Miss Sullivan. I think you ask too much, of her and yourself. God may not have meant Helen to have the—eyes you speak of.

Annie (*toneless*). I mean her to.

Keller (*curiously*). What is it to you?

(Annie's *head comes slowly up.*)

You make us see how we indulge her for our sake. Is the opposite true, for you?

Annie (*then*). Half a week?

Keller. An agreement *is* an agreement.

Annie. Mrs. Keller?

Kate (*simply*). I want her back.

(*A wait;* Annie *then lets her hands drop in surrender, and nods.*)

Keller. I'll send Viney over to help you pack.

Annie. Not until six o'clock. I have her till six o'clock.

Keller (*consenting*). Six o'clock. Come, Katie.

(Kate *leaving the window joins him around back, while* Keller *closes the door; they are shut out.*

Only the garden house is daylit now, and the light on it is narrowing down. Annie *stands watching* Helen *work* Belle's *claws. Then she settles beside them on her knees, and stops* Helen's *hand.*)

Annie (*gently*). No.

(*She shakes her head, with* Helen's *hand to her face, then spells.*)

Dog. D, o, g. Dog.

(*She touches* Helen's *hand to* Belle. Helen *dutifully pats the dog's head, and resumes spelling to its paw.*)

Not water.

(Annie *rolls to her feet, brings a tumbler of water back from the tray, and kneels with it, to seize* Helen's *hand and spell.*)

Here. Water. *Water.*

(*She thrusts* Helen's *hand into the tumbler.* Helen *lifts her hand out dripping, wipes it daintily on* Belle's *hide, and taking the tumbler from* Annie, *endeavors to thrust* Belle's *paw into it.* Annie *sits watching, wearily.*)

I don't know how to tell you. Not a soul in the world knows how to tell you. Helen, Helen.

(*She bends in compassion to touch her lips to* Helen's *temple, and instantly* Helen *pauses, her hands off the dog, her head slightly averted. The lights are still narrowing, and* Belle *slinks off. After a moment* Annie *sits back.*)

Yes, what's it to me? They're satisfied. Give them back their child and dog, both housebroken, everyone's satisfied. But me, and you.

(Helen's *hand comes out into the light, groping.*)

Reach. *Reach!*

(Annie *extending her own hand grips* Helen's; *the two hands are clasped, tense in the light, the rest of the room changing in shadow.)*

I wanted to teach you—oh, everything the earth is full of, Helen, everything on it that's ours for a wink and it's gone, and what we are on it, the— light we bring to it and leave behind in—words, why, you can see five thousand years back in a light of words, everything we feel, think, know—and share, in words, so not a soul is in darkness, or done with, even in the grave. And I know, I *know*, one word and I can—put the world in your hand— and whatever it is to me, I won't take less! How, how, how do I tell you that *this*—

(She spells.)

—means a *word*, and the word means this *thing*, wool?

(She thrusts the wool at Helen's hand; Helen sits, puzzled. Annie puts the crocheting aside.)

Or this—s, t, o, o, l—means this *thing*, stool?

(She claps Helen's palm to the stool. Helen waits, uncomprehending. Annie snatches up her napkin, spells:)

Napkin!

(She forces it on Helen's hand, waits, discards it, lifts a fold of the child's dress, spells:)

Dress!

(She lets it drop, spells:)

F, a, c, e, face!

(She draws Helen's hand to her cheek, and pressing it there, staring into the child's responseless eyes, hears the distant belfry begin to toll, slowly: one, two, three, four, five, six.

On the third stroke the lights stealing in around the garden house show us figures waiting. Viney, *the other servant,* Martha, Percy *at the drapes, and* James *on the dim porch.* Annie *and* Helen *remain, frozen. The chimes die away. Silently* Percy *moves the drape-rod back out of sight;* Viney *steps into the room—not using the door—and unmakes the bed; the other servant brings the wheelbarrow over, leaves it handy, rolls the bed off;* Viney *puts the bed linens on top of a waiting boxful of* Helen's *toys, and loads the box on the wheelbarrow;* Martha *and* Percy *take out the chairs, with the trayful, then the table; and* James, *coming down and into the room, lifts* Annie's *suitcase from its corner.* Viney *and the other servant load the remaining odds and ends on the wheelbarrow, and the servant wheels it off.* Viney *and the children departing leave only* James *in the room with* Annie *and* Helen. James *studies the two of them, without mockery, and then, quietly going to the door and opening it, bears the suitcase out, and housewards. He leaves the door open.*

Kate *steps into the doorway, and stands.* Annie *lifting her gaze from* Helen *sees her; she takes* Helen's *hand from her cheek, and returns it to the child's own, stroking it there twice, in her mother-sign, before spelling slowly into it:)*

M, o, t, h, e, r. Mother.

(Helen *with her hand free strokes her cheek, suddenly forlorn.* Annie *takes her hand again.)*

M, o, t, h—

(*But* Kate *is trembling with such impatience that her voice breaks from her, harsh.)*

Kate. Let her *come!*

(Annie *lifts* Helen *to her feet, with a turn, and gives her a little push. Now* Helen *begins groping, sensing something, trembling herself; and* Kate *falling one step in onto her knees clasps her, kissing her.* Helen *clutches her, tight as she can.* Kate *is inarticulate, choked, repeating* Helen's *name again and again. She wheels with her in her arms, to stumble away out the doorway;* Annie *stands unmoving, while* Kate *in a blind walk carries* Helen *like a baby behind the main house, out of view.*

Annie *is now alone on the stage. She turns, gazing around at the stripped room, bidding it silently farewell, impassively, like a defeated general on the deserted battlefield. All that remains is a stand with a basin of water; and here* Annie *takes up an eyecup, bathes each of her eyes, empties the eyecup, drops it in her purse, and tiredly locates her smoked glasses on the floor. The lights alter subtly; in the act of putting on her glasses* Annie *hears something that stops her, with head lifted. We hear it too, the voices out of the past, including her own now, in a whisper:*)

Boy's voice. You said we'd be together, forever— You promised, forever and—*Annie!*

Anagnos' voice. But that battle is dead and done with, why not let it stay buried?

Annie's voice (*whispering*). I think God must owe me a resurrection.

Anagnos' voice. What?

(*A pause, and* Annie *answers it herself, heavily.*)

Annie. And I owe God one.

Boy's voice. Forever and ever—

(Annie *shakes her head.*)

—forever, and ever, and—

(Annie *covers her ears.*)

—forever, and ever, and ever—

(*It pursues Annie; she flees to snatch up her purse, wheels to the doorway, and Keller is standing in it. The lights have lost their special color.*)

Keller. Miss—Annie.

(*He has an envelope in his fingers.*)

I've been waiting to give you this.

Annie (*after a breath*). What?

Keller. Your first month's salary.

(*He puts it in her hand.*)

With many more to come, I trust. It doesn't express what we feel, it doesn't pay our debt. For what you've done.

Annie. What have I done?

Keller. Taken a wild thing, and given us back a child.

Annie (*presently*). I taught her one thing, no. Don't do this, don't do that—

Keller. It's more than all of us could, in all the years we—

Annie. I wanted to teach her what language is. I wanted to teach her yes.

Keller. You will have time.

Annie. I don't know how. I know without it to do nothing but obey is—no gift, obedience without understanding is a—blindness, too. Is that all I've wished on her?

Keller (*gently*). No, no—

Annie. Maybe. I don't know what else to do. Simply go on, keep doing what I've done, and have—faith that inside she's— That inside it's waiting. Like water, underground. All I can do is keep on.

Keller. It's enough. For us.

Annie. You can help, Captain Keller.

Keller. How?

Annie. Even learning no has been at a cost. Of much trouble and pain. Don't undo it.

Keller. Why should we wish to—

Annie (*abruptly*). The world isn't an easy place for anyone, I don't want her just to obey but to let her have her way in everything is a lie, to *her*, I can't—

(*Her eyes fill, it takes her by surprise, and she laughs through it.*)

And I don't even love her, she's not my child! Well. You've got to stand between that lie and her.

Keller. We'll try.

Annie. Because *I* will. As long as you let me stay, that's one promise I'll keep.

Keller. Agreed. We've learned something too, I hope.

(*A pause*)

Won't you come now, to supper?

Annie. Yes.

(*She wags the envelope, ruefully.*)

Why doesn't God pay His debts each month?

Keller. I beg your pardon?

Annie. Nothing. I used to wonder how I could—

(*The lights are fading on them, simultaneously rising on the family room of the main house, where* Viney *is polishing glassware at the table set for dinner.)*

—earn a living.

Keller. Oh, you do.

Annie. I really do. Now the question is, can I survive it!

(Keller *smiles, offers his arm.*)

Keller. May I?

(Annie *takes it, and the lights lose them as he escorts her out.*

Now in the family room the rear door opens, and Helen *steps in. She stands a moment, then sniffs in one deep grateful breath, and her hands go out vigorously to familiar things, over the door panels, and to the chairs around the table, and over the silverware on the table, until she meets* Viney; *she pats her flank approvingly.*)

Viney. Oh, we glad to have you back too, prob'ly.

(Helen *hurries groping to the front door, opens and closes it, removes its key, opens and closes it again to be sure it is unlocked, gropes back to the rear door and repeats the procedure, removing its key and hugging herself gleefully.*

Aunt Ev *is next in by the rear door, with a relish tray; she bends to kiss* Helen's *cheek.* Helen *finds* Kate *behind her, and thrusts the keys at her.*)

Kate. What? Oh.

(*To* Ev)

Keys.

(*She pockets them, lets* Helen *feel them.*)

Yes, *I'll* keep the keys. I think we've had enough of locked doors, too.

(James, *having earlier put* Annie's *suitcase inside her door upstairs and taken himself out of view around the corner, now reappears and comes down the stairs as* Annie *and* Keller *mount the porch steps. Following them into the family room, he pats* Annie's *hair in passing, rather to her surprise.*)

James. Evening, general.

(*He takes his own chair opposite.*

Viney *bears the empty water pitcher out to the porch. The remaining suggestion of garden house is gone now, and the water pump is unobstructed;* Viney *pumps water into the pitcher.*

Kate *surveying the table breaks the silence.*)

Kate. Will you say grace, Jimmie?

(*They bow their heads, except for* Helen, *who palms her empty plate and then reaches to be sure her mother is there.* James *considers a moment, glances across at* Annie, *lowers his head again, and obliges.*)

James (*lightly*). And Jacob was left alone, and wrestled with an angel until the breaking of the day; and the hollow of Jacob's thigh was out of joint, as he wrestled with him; and the angel said, Let me go, for the day breaketh. And Jacob said, I will not let thee go, except thou bless me. Amen.

(Annie *has lifted her eyes suspiciously at* James, *who winks expressionlessly and inclines his head to* Helen.)

Oh, you angel.

(*The others lift their faces;* Viney *returns with the pitcher, setting it down near* Kate, *then goes out the rear door; and* Annie *puts a napkin around* Helen.)

Aunt Ev. That's a very strange grace, James.

Keller. Will you start the muffins, Ev?

James. It's from the Good Book, isn't it?

Aunt Ev (*passing a plate*). Well, of course it is. Didn't you know?

James. Yes, I knew.

Keller (*serving*). Ham, Miss Annie?

Annie. Please.

Aunt Ev. Then why ask?

James. I meant it *is* from the Good Book, and therefore a fitting grace.

Aunt Ev. Well. I don't know about *that*.

Kate (*with the pitcher*). Miss Annie?

Annie. Thank you.

Aunt Ev. There's an awful *lot* of things in the Good Book that I wouldn't care to hear just before eating.

(*When* Annie *reaches for the pitcher,* Helen *removes her napkin and drops it to the floor.* Annie *is filling* Helen's *glass when she notices it; she considers* Helen's *bland expression a moment, then bends, retrieves it, and tucks it around* Helen's *neck again.*)

James. Well, fitting in the sense that Jacob's thigh was out of joint, and so is this piggie's.

Aunt Ev. I declare, James—

Kate. Pickles, Aunt Ev?

Aunt Ev. Oh, I should say so, you know my opinion of your pickles—

Kate. This is the end of them, I'm afraid. I didn't put up nearly enough last summer, this year I intend to—

(*She interrupts herself, seeing* Helen *deliberately lift off her napkin and drop it again to the floor. She bends to retrieve it, but* Annie *stops her arm.*)

Keller (*not noticing*). Reverend looked in at the office today to complain his hens have stopped laying. Poor fellow, *he* was out of joint, all he could—

(*He stops too, to frown down the table at* Kate, Helen, *and* Annie *in turn, all suspended in mid-motion.*)

James (*not noticing*). I've always suspected those hens.

Aunt Ev. Of what?

James. I think they're Papist. Has he tried—

(*He stops, too, following* Keller's *eyes.* Annie *now stops to pick the napkin up.*)

Aunt Ev. James, now you're pulling my—lower extremity, the first thing you know we'll be—

(*She stops, too, hearing herself in the silence.* Annie, *with everyone now watching, for the third time puts the napkin on* Helen. Helen *yanks it off, and throws it down.* Annie *rises, lifts* Helen's *plate, and bears it away.* Helen, *feeling it gone, slides down and commences to kick up under the table; the dishes jump.* Annie *contemplates this for a moment, then coming back takes* Helen's *wrists firmly and swings her off the chair.* Helen *struggling gets one hand free, and catches at her mother's skirt; when* Kate *takes her by the shoulders,* Helen *hangs quiet.*)

Kate. Miss Annie.

Annie. No.

Kate (*a pause*). It's a very special day.

Annie (*grimly*). It will be, when I give in to that.

(*She tries to disengage* Helen's *hand;* Kate *lays hers on* Annie's.)

Kate. Please. I've hardly had a chance to welcome her home—

Annie. Captain Keller.

Keller (*embarrassed*). Oh. Katie, we—had a little talk, Miss Annie feels that if we indulge Helen in these—

Aunt Ev. But what's the child done?

Annie. She's learned not to throw things on the floor and kick. It took us the best part of two weeks and—

Aunt Ev. But only a napkin, it's not as if it were breakable!

Annie. And everything she's learned *is?* Mrs. Keller, I don't think we should—play tug-of-war for her, either give her to me or you keep her from kicking.

Kate. What do you wish to do?

Annie. Let me take her from the table.

Aunt Ev. Oh, let her stay, my goodness, she's only a child, she doesn't have to wear a napkin if she doesn't want to her first evening—

Annie (*level*). And ask outsiders not to interfere.

Aunt Ev (*astonished*). Out—outsi— I'm the child's *aunt!*

Kate (*distressed*). Will once hurt so much, Miss Annie? I've—made all Helen's favorite foods, tonight.

(*A pause*)

Keller (*gently*). It's a homecoming party, Miss Annie.

(Annie *after a moment releases* Helen. *But she cannot accept it, at her own chair she shakes her head and turns back, intent on* Kate.)

Annie. She's testing you. You realize?

James (*to* Annie). She's testing you.

Keller. Jimmie, be quiet.

(James *sits, tense.*)

Now she's home, naturally she—

Annie. And wants to see what will happen. At your hands. I said it was my main worry, is this what you promised me not half an hour ago?

Keller (*reasonably*). But she's *not* kicking, now—

Annie. And not learning not to. Mrs. Keller, teaching her is bound to be painful, to everyone. I know it hurts to watch, but she'll live up to just what you demand of her, and no more.

James (*palely*). She's testing *you*.

Keller (*testily*). Jimmie.

James. I have an opinion, I think I should—

Keller. No one's interested in hearing your opinion.

Annie. *I'm* interested, of course she's testing me. Let me keep her to what she's learned and she'll go on learning from me. Take her out of my hands and it all comes apart.

(Kate *closes her eyes, digesting it;* Annie *sits again, with a brief comment for her.*)

Be bountiful, it's at her expense.

(*She turns to* James, *flatly.*)

Please pass me more of—her favorite foods.

(*Then* Kate *lifts* Helen's *hand, and turning her toward* Annie, *surrenders her;* Helen *makes for her own chair.*)

Kate (*low*). Take her, Miss Annie.

Annie (*then*). Thank you.

(*But the moment* Annie *rising reaches for her hand,* Helen *begins to fight and kick, clutching to the tablecloth, and uttering laments.* Annie *again tries to loosen her hand, and* Keller *rises.*)

Keller (*tolerant*). I'm afraid you're the difficulty, Miss Annie. Now I'll keep her to what she's learned, you're quite right there—

(*He takes* Helen's *hands from* Annie, *pats them;* Helen *quiets down.*)

—but I don't see that we need send her from the table, after all, she's the guest of honor. Bring her plate back.

Annie. If she was a seeing child, none of you would tolerate one—

Keller. Well, she's not, I think some compromise is called for. Bring her plate, please.

(Annie's *jaw sets, but she restores the plate, while* Keller *fastens the napkin around* Helen's *neck; she permits it.*)

There. It's not unnatural, most of us take some aversion to our teachers, and occasionally another hand can smooth things out.

(*He puts a fork in* Helen's *hand;* Helen *takes it. Genially:*)

Now. Shall we start all over?

(*He goes back around the table, and sits.* Annie *stands watching.* Helen *is motionless, thinking things through, until with a wicked glee she deliberately flings the fork on the floor. After another moment she plunges her hand into her food, and crams a fistful into her mouth.*)

James (*wearily*). I think we've started all over—

(Keller *shoots a glare at him, as* Helen *plunges her other hand into* Annie's *plate.* Annie *at once moves in, to grasp her wrist, and* Helen *flinging out a hand encounters the pitcher; she swings with it at* Annie; Annie *falling back blocks it with an elbow, but the water flies over her dress.* Annie *gets her breath, then snatches the pitcher away in one hand, hoists* Helen *up bodily under the other arm, and starts to carry her out, kicking.* Keller *stands.*)

Annie (*savagely polite*). Don't get up!

Keller. Where are you going?

Annie. Don't smooth anything else out for me, don't interfere in any way! I treat her like a seeing child because I *ask* her to see, I *expect* her to see, don't undo what I do!

Keller. Where are you taking her?

Annie. To make her fill this pitcher again!

(*She thrusts out with* Helen *under her arm, but* Helen *escapes up the stairs and* Annie *runs after her.* Keller *stands rigid.* Aunt Ev *is astounded.*)

Aunt Ev. You let her speak to you like that, Arthur? A creature who *works* for you?

Keller (*angrily*). No. I don't.

(*He is starting after* Annie *when* James, *on his feet with shaky resolve, interposes his chair between them in* Keller's *path.*)

James. Let her go.

Keller. What!

James (*a swallow*). I said—let her go. She's right.

(Keller *glares at the chair and him.* James *takes a deep breath, then headlong:*)

She's right, Kate's right, I'm right, and you're wrong. If you drive her away from here it will be over my dead—chair, has it never occurred to you that on one occasion you might be consummately wrong?

(Keller's *stare is unbelieving, even a little fascinated.* Kate *rises in trepidation, to mediate.*)

Kate. Captain.

(Keller *stops her with his raised hand; his eyes stay on* James's *pale face, for a long hold. When he finally finds his voice, it is gruff.*)

Keller. Sit down, everyone.

(*He sits.* Kate *sits.* James *holds onto his chair.* Keller *speaks mildly.*)

Please sit down, Jimmie.

(James *sits, and a moveless silence prevails;* Keller's *eyes do not leave him.*

Annie *has pulled* Helen *downstairs again by one hand, the pitcher in her other hand, down the porch steps, and across the yard to the pump. She puts* Helen's *hand on the pump handle, grimly.*)

Annie. All right. Pump.

(Helen *touches her cheek, waits uncertainly.*)

No, she's not here. Pump!

(*She forces* Helen's *hand to work the handle, then lets go. And* Helen *obeys. She pumps till the water comes, then* Annie *puts the pitcher in her other hand and guides it under the spout, and the water tumbling half into and half around the pitcher douses* Helen's *hand.* Annie *takes over the handle to keep water coming, and does automatically what she has done so many times before, spells into* Helen's *free palm:)*

Water. W, a, t, e, r. *Water.* It has a—*name*—

(*And now the miracle happens.* Helen *drops the pitcher on the slab under the spout, it shatters. She stands transfixed.* Annie *freezes on the pump handle: there is a change in the sundown light, and with it a change in* Helen's *face, some light coming into it we have never seen there, some struggle in the depths behind it; and her lips tremble, trying to remember something the muscles around them once knew, till at last it finds its way out, painfully, a baby sound buried under the debris of years of dumbness.*)

Helen. Wah. Wah.

(*And again, with great effort*)

Wah. Wah.

(Helen *plunges her hand into the dwindling water, spells into her own palm. Then she gropes frantically,* Annie *reaches for her hand, and* Helen *spells into* Annie's *hand.*)

Annie (*whispering*). Yes.

(Helen *spells into it again.*)

Yes!

(Helen *grabs at the handle, pumps for more water, plunges her hand into its spurt and grabs* Annie's *to spell it again.*)

Yes! Oh, my dear—

(*She falls to her knees to clasp* Helen's *hand, but* Helen *pulls it free, stands almost bewildered, then drops to the ground, pats it swiftly, holds up her palm, imperious.* Annie *spells into it:*)

Ground.

(Helen *spells it back.*)

Yes!

(Helen *whirls to the pump, pats it, holds up her palm, and* Annie *spells into it.*)

Pump.

(Helen *spells it back.*)

Yes! Yes!

(*Now* Helen *is in such an excitement she is possessed, wild, trembling, cannot be still, turns, runs, falls on the porch steps, claps it, reaches out her palm, and* Annie *is at it instantly to spell:*)

Step.

(Helen *has no time to spell back now, she whirls groping, to touch anything, encounters the trellis, shakes it, thrusts out her palm, and* Annie *while spelling to her cries wildly at the house.*)

Trellis. Mrs. Keller! *Mrs. Keller!*

(*Inside,* Kate *starts to her feet.* Helen *scrambles back onto the porch, groping, and finds the bell string, tugs it; the bell rings, the distant chimes begin tolling the hour, all the bells in town seem to break into speech while* Helen *reaches out and* Annie *spells feverishly into her hand.* Kate *hurries out, with* Keller *after her;* Aunt Ev *is on her feet, to peer out the window; only* James *remains at the table, and with a napkin wipes his damp brow. From up right and left the servants—* Viney, *the two Negro children, the other servant—run in, and stand watching from a distance as* Helen, *ringing the bell, with her other hand encounters her mother's skirt; when she throws a hand out,* Annie *spells into it.*)

Mother.

(Keller *now seizes* Helen's *hand, she touches him, gestures a hand, and* Annie *again spells:*)

Papa— She *knows!*

(Kate *and* Keller *go to their knees, stammering, clutching* Helen *to them, and* Annie *steps unsteadily back to watch the threesome,* Helen *spelling wildly into* Kate's *hand, then into* Keller's, Kate *spelling back into* Helen's; *they cannot keep their hands off her, and rock her in their clasp.*

Then Helen *gropes, feels nothing, turns all around, pulls free, and comes with both hands groping, to find* Annie. *She encounters* Annie's *thighs,* Annie *kneels to her,* Helen's *hand pats* Annie's *cheek impatiently, points a finger, and waits; and* Annie *spells into it:*)

Teacher.

(Helen *spells it back, slowly;* Annie *nods.*)

Teacher.

(*She holds* Helen's *hand to her cheek. Presently* Helen *withdraws it, not jerkily, only with reserve, and retreats a step. She stands thinking it over, then turns again and stumbles back to her parents. They try to embrace her, but she has something else in mind, it is to get the keys, and she hits* Kate's *pocket until* Kate *digs them out for her.*

Annie *with her own load of emotion has retreated, her back turned, toward the pump, to sit;* Kate *moves to* Helen, *touches her hand questioningly, and* Helen *spells a word to her.* Kate *comprehends it, their first act of verbal communication, and she can hardly utter the word aloud, in wonder, gratitude, and deprivation; it is a moment in which she simultaneously finds and loses a child.*)

Kate. Teacher?

(Annie *turns; and* Kate, *facing* Helen *in her direction by the shoulders, holds her back, holds her back, and then relinquishes her.* Helen *feels her way across the yard, rather* shyly, and when her moving hands touch Annie's *skirt she stops. Then she holds out the keys and places them in Annie's hand. For a moment neither of them moves. Then* Helen *slides into* Annie's *arms, and lifting away her smoked glasses, kisses her on the cheek.* Annie *gathers her in.*

Kate *torn both ways turns from this, gestures the servants off, and makes her way into the house, on* Keller's *arm. The servants go, in separate directions.*

The lights are half down now, except over the pump. Annie *and* Helen *are here, alone in the yard.* Annie *has found* Helen's *hand, almost without knowing it, and she spells slowly into it, her voice unsteady, whispering:)*

Annie. I, love, Helen.

(She clutches the child to her, tight this time, not spelling, whispering into her hair.)

Forever, and—

(She stops. The lights over the pump are taking on the color of the past, and it brings Annie's *head up, her eyes opening, in fear; and as slowly as though drawn she rises, to listen, with her hand on* Helen's *shoulders. She waits, waits, listening with ears and eyes both, slowly here, slowly there, and hears only silence. There are no voices. The color passes on, and when her eyes come back to* Helen *she can breathe the end of her phrase without fear:)*

—ever.

(In the family room Kate *has stood over the table, staring at* Helen's *plate, with* Keller *at her shoulder; now* James *takes a step to move her chair in, and* Kate *sits, with head erect, and* Keller *inclines his head to* James; *so it is* Aunt Ev, *hesitant, and rather humble, who moves to the door.*

Outside Helen *tugs at* Annie's *hand, and* Annie *comes with it.* Helen *pulls her toward the house; and hand in hand, they cross the yard, and ascend the porch steps, in the rising lights, to where* Aunt Ev *is holding the door open for them.*

The curtain ends the play.)

Related Readings

CONTENTS

from Three Days to See

by Helen Keller

The 1887 incident at the water pump sparked Helen Keller's lifelong desire to touch and know the world. News of the young girl's incredible breakthroughs eventually brought her worldwide attention, which Helen used to teach some lessons of her own. Throughout Helen's adult life, she wrote, lectured, and traveled tirelessly to make others aware of the capabilities and needs of the physically disabled. She also shared many strong opinions. Consider how Helen's message in this essay from the 1930s is relevant to readers of today.

Only the deaf appreciate hearing; only the blind realize the manifold blessings that lie in sight. Particularly does this observation apply to those who have lost sight and hearing in adult life. But those who have never suffered impairment of sight or hearing seldom make the fullest use of these blessed faculties. Their eyes and ears take in all sights and sounds hazily, without concentration, and with little appreciation. It is the same old story of not being grateful for what we have until we lose it, of not being conscious of health until we are ill.

I have often thought it would be a blessing if each human being were stricken blind and deaf for a few days at some time during his or her early adult life. Darkness would make people more appreciative of sight; silence would teach them the joys of sound.

Now and then I have tested my seeing friends to

discover what they see. Recently I was visited by a very good friend who had just returned from a long walk in the woods, and I asked her what she had observed. "Nothing in particular," she replied. I might have been incredulous had I not been accustomed to such responses, for long ago I became convinced that the seeing see little.

How was it possible, I asked myself, to walk for an hour through the woods and see nothing worthy of note? I who cannot see, find hundreds of things to interest me through mere touch. I feel the delicate symmetry of a leaf. I pass my hands lovingly about the smooth skin of a silver birch, or the rough, shaggy bark of a pine. In spring I touch the branches of trees hopefully in search of a bud, the first sign of awakening Nature after the winter's sleep. I feel the delightful, velvety texture of a flower, and discover its remarkable convolutions; and something of the miracle of Nature is revealed to me. Occasionally, if I am very fortunate, I place my hand gently on a small tree and feel the happy quiver of a bird in full song. I am delighted to have the cool waters of a brook rush through my open fingers. To me, a lush carpet of pine needles or spongy grass is more welcome than the most luxurious Persian rug. To me, the pageant of seasons is a thrilling and unending drama, the action of which streams through my fingertips.

At times my heart cries out with longing to see all these things. If I can get so much pleasure from mere touch, how much more beauty must be revealed by sight? Yet those who have eyes apparently see little. The panorama of color and action that fills the world is taken for granted. It is human, perhaps, to appreciate little of that which we have and to long for that which we have not; but it is a great pity that in the world of light, the gift of sight is used only as a mere convenience rather than as a means of adding fullness to life.

If I were the president of a university, I should establish a compulsory course in "How To Use Your Eyes." The professor would try to show the pupils how they could add joy to their lives by really seeing what passes unnoticed before them. He or she would try to awake their dormant and sluggish faculties.

Perhaps I can best illustrate by imagining what I should most like to see if I were given the use of my eyes, say, for just three days. And while I am imagining, suppose you, too, set your mind to work on the problem of how you would use your own eyes if you had only three more days to see. If, with the oncoming darkness of the third night you knew that the sun would never rise for you again, how would you spend those three precious, intervening days? What would you most want to let your gaze rest upon?

I, naturally, should want most to see the things that have become dear to me through my years of darkness. You, too, would want to let your eyes rest long on the things that have become dear to you, so that you could take the memory of them with you into the night that loomed before you.

If, by some miracle, I were granted three seeing days, to be followed by a relapse into darkness, I should want to see the people whose kindness and gentleness and companionship have made my life worth living. First I should like to gaze long upon the face of my dear teacher, Mrs. Anna Sullivan Macy, who came to me when I was a child and opened the outer world to me. I should want not merely to see the outline of her face, so that I could cherish it in my memory, but to study that face and find in it the living evidence of the sympathetic tenderness and patience with which she accomplished the difficult task of my education. I should like to see in her eyes that strength of character that has enabled her to stand firm in the face of difficulties, and that compassion for all humanity that she has revealed to me so often.

I do not know what it is to see into the heart of a friend through that "window of the soul," the eye. I can only "see" through my fingertips the outline of a face. I can detect laughter, sorrow, and many other obvious emotions. I know my friends from the feel of their faces. But I cannot really picture their personalities by touch. I know their personalities, of course, through other means, through the thoughts they express to me, through whatever of their actions are revealed to me. But I am denied that deeper understanding of them that I am sure would come through sight of them, through watching their reactions to various expressed thoughts and circumstances, through noting the immediate and fleeting reactions of their eyes and countenance.

Friends who are near to me I know well, because through the months and years they reveal themselves to me in all their phases; but of casual friends I have only an incomplete impression, an impression gained from a handclasp, from spoken words that I take from their lips with my fingertips, or which they tap into the palm of my hand.

How much easier, how much more satisfying it is for you who can see to grasp quickly the essential qualities of another person by watching the subtleties of expression, the quiver of a muscle, the flutter of a hand. But does it ever occur to you to use your sight to see into the inner nature of a friend or acquaintance? Do not most of you seeing people grasp casually the outward features of a face and let it go at that?

For instance, can you describe accurately the faces of five good friends? Some of you can, but many cannot. As an experiment, I have questioned husbands of long standing about the color of their wives' eyes, and often they express embarrassed confusion and admit that they do not know. And, incidentally, it is a chronic complaint of wives that their husbands do not notice new dresses, new hats, and changes in household arrangements.

The eyes of seeing persons soon become accustomed to the routine of their surroundings, and they actually see only the startling and spectacular. But even in viewing the most spectacular sights, the eyes are lazy. Court records reveal every day how inaccurately "eyewitnesses" see. A given event will be "seen" in several different ways by as many witnesses. Some see more than others, but few see everything that is within the range of their vision.

Oh, the things that I should see if I had the power of sight for just three days!

The first day would be a busy one. I should call to me all my dear friends and look long into their faces, imprinting upon my mind the outward evidence of the beauty that is within them. I should let my eyes rest, too, on the face of a baby, so that I could catch a vision of the eager, innocent beauty that precedes the individual's consciousness of the conflicts that life develops.

And I should like to look into the loyal, trusting eyes of my dogs—the grave, canny little Scottie, Darkie, and the stalwart, understanding Great Dane, Helga, whose warm, tender, and playful friendships are so comforting to me.

On that busy first day I should also view the small, simple things of my home. I want to see the warm colors in the rugs under my feet, the pictures on the walls, the intimate trifles that transform a house into a home. My eyes would rest respectfully on the books in raised type that I have read, but they would be more eagerly interested in the printed books that seeing people can read; for during the long night of my life the books I have read and those that have been read to me have built themselves into a great, shining lighthouse, revealing to me the deepest channels of human life and the human spirit.

In the afternoon of that first seeing day, I should take a long walk in the woods and intoxicate my eyes on the beauties of the world of Nature, trying desperately to absorb in a few hours the vast splendor that is constantly unfolding itself to those who can see. On the way home from my woodland jaunt, my path would lie near a farm, so that I might see the patient horses plowing in the field (perhaps I should see only a tractor!) and the serene content of people living close to the soil. And I should pray for the glory of a colorful sunset.

When dusk had fallen, I should experience the double delight of being able to see by artificial light, which the human genius has created to extend the power of sight when Nature decrees darkness.

In the night of that first day of sight, I should not be able to sleep, so full would be my mind of the memories of the day.

I who am blind can give one hint to those who see—one admonition to those who would make full use of the gift of sight: Use your eyes as if tomorrow you would be stricken blind. And the same method can be applied to the other senses. Hear the music of voices, the song of a bird, the mighty strains of an orchestra, as if you would be stricken deaf tomorrow. Touch each object you want to touch as if tomorrow your tactile sense would fail. Smell the perfume of flowers, taste with relish each morsel, as if tomorrow you could never smell and taste again. Make the most of every sense; glory in all facets of pleasure and beauty that the world reveals to you through the several means of contact that Nature provides. But of all the senses, I am sure that sight must be the most delightful.

Darkness at Noon

by Harold Krents

This essay focuses on the everyday occurrences in the life of Harold Krents, a person who was born blind in the 1940s. How might Helen Keller have responded to this account of Krents's experiences?

Blind from birth, I have never had the opportunity to see myself and have been completely dependent on the image I create in the eye of the observer. To date it has not been narcissistic.

There are those who assume that since I can't see, I obviously also cannot hear. Very often people will converse with me at the top of their lungs, enunciating each word very carefully. Conversely, people will also often whisper, assuming that since my eyes don't work, my ears don't either.

For example, when I go to the airport and ask the ticket agent for assistance to the plane, he or she will invariably pick up the phone, call a ground hostess and whisper: "Hi, Jane, we've got a 76 here." I have concluded that the word "blind" is not used for one of two reasons: Either they fear that if the dread word is spoken, the ticket agent's retina will immediately detach, or they are reluctant to inform me of my condition of which I may not have been previously aware.

On the other hand, others know that of course I can hear, but believe that I can't talk. Often, therefore, when my wife and I go out to dinner, a waiter or waitress will ask Kit if "*he* would like a drink" to which I respond that "indeed *he* would."

This point was graphically driven home to me while we were in England. I had been given a year's leave of absence from my Washington law firm to study for a diploma in law degree at Oxford University. During the year I became ill and was hospitalized. Immediately after admission, I was wheeled down to the X-ray room. Just at the door sat an elderly woman—elderly I would judge from the sound of her voice. "What is his name?" the woman asked the orderly who had been wheeling me.

"What's your name?" the orderly repeated to me.

"Harold Krents," I replied.

"Harold Krents," he repeated.

"When was he born?"

"When were you born?"

"Nov. 5, 1944," I responded.

"Nov. 5, 1944," the orderly intoned.

This procedure continued for approximately five minutes at which point even my saint-like disposition deserted me. "Look," I finally blurted out, "this is absolutely ridiculous. Okay, granted I can't see, but it's got to have become pretty clear to both of you that I don't need an interpreter."

"He says he doesn't need an interpreter," the orderly reported to the woman.

The toughest misconception of all is the view that because I can't see, I can't work. I was turned down by over forty law firms because of my blindness, even though my qualifications included a cum laude degree from Harvard College and a good ranking in my Harvard Law School class.

The attempt to find employment, the continuous frustration of being told that it was impossible for a blind person to practice law, the rejection letters, not based on my lack of ability but rather on my disability, will always remain one of the most disillusioning experiences of my life.

Fortunately, this view of limitation and exclusion is beginning to change. On April 16, the Department of Labor issued regulations that mandate equal-employment opportunities for the handicapped. By and large, the business community's response to offering employment to the disabled has been enthusiastic.

I therefore look forward to the day, with the expectation that it is certain to come, when employers will view their handicapped workers as a little child did me years ago when my family still lived in Scarsdale.

I was playing basketball with my father in our backyard according to procedures we had developed. My father would stand beneath the hoop, shout, and I would shoot over his head at the basket attached to our garage. Our next-door neighbor, aged five, wandered over into our yard with a playmate. "He's blind," our neighbor whispered to her friend in a voice that could be heard distinctly by Dad and me. Dad shot and missed; I did the same. Dad hit the rim; I missed entirely; Dad shot and missed the garage entirely. "Which one is blind?" whispered back the little friend.

I would hope that in the near future when a plant manager is touring the factory with the foreman and comes upon a handicapped and nonhandicapped person working together, his comment after watching them work will be, "Which one is disabled?"

And Sarah Laughed

by Joanne Greenberg

When Annie Sullivan arrives at the Keller home in Tuscumbia, Alabama, the household has no idea what new challenges lie ahead. In this story, Sarah awaits the arrival of her brand-new daughter-in-law. Discover what happens when Sarah's comfortable notions about her world no longer seem so comfortable.

She went to the window every fifteen minutes to see if they were coming. They would be taking the new highway cutoff; it would bring them past the south side of the farm; past the unused, dilapidated outbuildings instead of the orchards and fields that were now full and green. It would look like a poor place to the new bride. Her first impression of their farm would be of age and bleached-out, dried-out buildings on which the doors hung open like a row of gaping mouths that said nothing.

All day, Sarah had gone about her work clumsy with eagerness and hesitant with dread, picking up utensils to forget them in holding, finding them two minutes later a surprise in her hand. She had been planning and working ever since Abel wrote to them from Chicago that he was coming home with a wife. Everything should have been clean and orderly. She wanted the bride to know as soon as she walked inside what kind of woman Abel's mother was—to feel, without a word having to be said, the house's dignity, honesty, simplicity, and love. But the spring cleaning had been late, and Alma Yoder had gotten sick—Sarah had had to go over to the Yoders and help out.

Now she looked around and saw that it was no use trying to have everything ready in time. Abel and his bride would be coming any minute. If she didn't want to get caught shedding tears of frustration, she'd better get herself under control. She stepped over the pile of clothes still unsorted for the laundry and went out on the back porch.

The sky was blue and silent, but as she watched, a bird passed over the fields crying. The garden spread out before her, displaying its varying greens. Beyond it, along the creek, there was a row of poplars. It always calmed her to look at them. She looked today. She and Matthew had planted those trees. They stood thirty feet high now, stately as figures in a procession. Once—only once and many years ago—she had tried to describe in words the sounds that the wind made as it combed those trees on its way west. The little boy to whom she had spoken was a grown man now, and he was bringing home a wife. *Married. . . .*

Ever since he had written to tell them he was coming with his bride, Sarah had been going back in her mind to the days when she and Matthew were bride and groom and then mother and father. Until now, it hadn't seemed so long ago. Her life had flowed on past her, blurring the early days with Matthew when this farm was strange and new to her and when the silence of it was sharp and bitter like pain, not dulled and familiar like an echo of old age.

Matthew hadn't changed much. He was a tall, lean man, but he had had a boy's spareness then. She remembered how his smile came, wavered and went uncertainly, but how his eyes had never left her. He followed everything with his eyes. Matthew had always been a silent man; his face was expressionless and his body stiff with reticence, but his eyes had sought her out eagerly and held her and she had been warm in his look.

Sarah and Matthew had always known each other—their families had been neighbors. Sarah was a plain girl, a serious "decent" girl. Not many of the young men asked her out, and when Matthew did and did again, her parents had been pleased. Her father told her that Matthew was a good man, as steady as any woman could want. He came from honest, hardworking people and he would prosper any farm he had. Her mother spoke shyly of how his eyes woke when Sarah came into the room, and how they followed her. If she married him, her life would be full of the things she knew and loved, an easy, familiar world with her parents' farm not two miles down the road. But no one wanted to mention the one thing that worried Sarah: the fact that Matthew was deaf. It was what stopped her from saying yes right away; she loved him, but she was worried about his deafness. The things she feared about it were the practical things: a fall or a fire when he wouldn't hear her cry for help. Only long after she had put those fears aside and moved the scant two miles into his different world, did she realize that the things she had feared were the wrong things.

Now they had been married for twenty-five years. It was a good marriage—good enough. Matthew was generous, strong, and loving. The farm prospered. His silence made him seem more patient, and because she became more silent also, their neighbors saw in them the dignity and strength of two people who do not rail against misfortune, who were beyond trivial talk and gossip; whose lives needed no words. Over the years of help given and meetings attended, people noticed how little they needed to say. Only Sarah's friend Luita knew that in the beginning, when they were first married, they had written yearning notes to each other. But Luita didn't know that the notes also were mute. Sarah had never shown them to anyone, although she kept them all, and sometimes she would go up and get the box out of her closet and read them over. She had saved every scrap, from questions about the eggs to the tattered note he had left beside his plate on their first anniversary. He had written it when she was busy at the stove and then he'd gone out and she hadn't seen it until she cleared the table.

The note said: "I love you derest wife Sarah. I pray you have happy day all day your life."

When she wanted to tell him something, she spoke to him slowly, facing him, and he took the words as they formed on her lips. His speaking voice was thick and hard to understand and he perceived that it was unpleasant. He didn't like to use it. When he had to say something, he used his odd, grunting tone, and she came to understand what he said. If she ever hungered for laughter from him or the little meaningless talk that confirms existence and affection, she told herself angrily that Matthew talked through his work. Words die in the air; they can be turned one way or another, but Matthew's work prayed and laughed for him. He took good care of her and the boys, and they idolized him. Surely that counted more than all the words— words that meant and didn't mean—behind which people could hide.

Over the years she seldom noticed her own increasing silence, and there were times when his tenderness, which was always given without words, seemed to her to make his silence beautiful.

She thought of the morning she had come downstairs feeling heavy and off balance with her first pregnancy—with Abel. She had gone to the kitchen to begin the day, taking the coffeepot down and beginning to fill it when her eye caught something on the kitchen table. For a minute she looked around in confusion. They had already laid away what the baby would need: diapers, little shirts and bedding, all folded away in the drawer upstairs, but here on the table was a bounty of cloth, all planned and scrimped for and bought from careful, careful study of the catalogue—yards of patterned flannel and plissé, coat wool and bright red corduroy. Sixteen yards of yellow ribbon for bindings. Under the coat wool was cloth Matthew had chosen for her; blue with a little gray figure. It was silk, and there was a card on which was rolled precisely enough lace edging for her collar and sleeves. All the long studying and careful planning, all in silence.

She had run upstairs and thanked him and hugged him, but it was no use showing delight with words, making plans, matching cloth and figuring which pieces would be for the jacket and which for sleepers. Most wives used such fussing to tell their husbands how much they thought of their gifts. But Matthew's silence was her silence too.

When he had left to go to the orchard after breakfast that morning, she had gone to their room and stuffed her ears with cotton, trying to understand the world as it must be to him, with no sound. The cotton dulled the outside noises a little, but it only magnified all the noises in her head. Scratching her cheek caused a roar like a downpour of rain; her own voice was like thunder. She knew Matthew could not hear his own voice in his head. She could not be deaf as he was deaf. She could not know such silence ever.

So she found herself talking to the baby inside her, telling it the things she would have told Matthew, the idle daily things: Didn't Margaret Amson look peaked in town? Wasn't it a shame the drugstore had stopped stocking lump alum—her pickles wouldn't be the same.

Abel was a good baby. He had Matthew's great eyes and gentle ways. She chattered to him all day, looking forward to his growing up, when there would be confidences between them. She looked to the time when he would have his own picture of the world, and with that keen hunger and hope she had a kind of late blooming into a beauty that made people in town turn to look at her when she passed in the street holding the baby in the fine clothes she had made for him. She took Abel everywhere, and came to know a pride that was very new to her, a plain girl from a modest family who had married a neighbor boy. When they went to town, they always stopped over to see Matthew's parents and her mother.

Mama had moved to town after Pa died. Of course they had offered to have Mama come and live with them, but Sarah was glad she had gone to a little place in town, living where there were people she knew and things happening right outside her door. Sarah remembered them visiting on a certain spring day, all sitting in Mama's new front room. They sat uncomfortably in the genteel chairs, and Abel crawled around on the floor as the women talked, looking up every now and then for his father's nod of approval. After a while he went to catch the sunlight that was glancing off a crystal nut dish and scattering rainbow bands on the floor. Sarah smiled down at him. She too had a radiance, and, for the first time in her life, she knew it. She was wearing the dress she had made from Matthew's cloth—it became her and she knew that too, so she gave her joy freely as she traded news with Mama.

Suddenly they heard the fire bell ringing up on the hill. She caught Matthew's eye and mouthed, "Fire engines," pointing uphill to the firehouse. He nodded.

In the next minutes there was the strident, off-key blare as every single one of Arcadia's volunteer firemen—his car horn plugged with a matchstick and his duty before him—drove hellbent for the firehouse in an ecstasy of bell and siren. In a minute the ding-ding-ding-ding careened in deafening, happy privilege through every red light in town.

"Big bunch of boys!" Mama laughed. "You can count two Saturdays in good weather when they don't have a fire, and that's during the hunting season!"

They laughed. Then Sarah looked down at Abel, who was still trying to catch the wonderful colors. A madhouse of bells, horns, screaming sirens had gone right past them and he hadn't cried, he hadn't looked, he hadn't turned. Sarah twisted her head sharply away and screamed to the china cats on the whatnot shelf as loud as she could, but Abel's eyes only flickered to the movement and then went back to the sun and its colors.

Mama whispered, "Oh, my dear God!"

Sarah began to cry bitterly, uncontrollably, while her husband and son looked on, confused, embarrassed, unknowing.

The silence drew itself over the seasons and the seasons layered into years. Abel was a good boy; Matthew was a good man.

Later, Rutherford, Lindsay, and Franklin Delano came. They too were silent. Hereditary nerve deafness was rare, the doctors all said. The boys might marry and produce deaf children, but it was not likely. When they started to school, the administrators and teachers told her that the boys would be taught specially to read lips and to speak. They would not be "abnormal," she was told. Nothing would show their handicap, and with training no one need know that they were deaf. But the boys seldom used their lifeless voices to call to their friends; they seldom joined games unless they were forced to join. No one but their mother understood their speech. No teacher could stop all the jumping, turning, gum-chewing schoolboys, or remember herself to face front from the blackboard to the sound-closed boys. The lip-reading exercises never seemed to make plain differences—"man," "pan," "began."

But the boys had work and pride in the farm. The seasons varied their silence with colors—crows flocked in the snowy fields in winter, and tones of golden wheat darkened across acres of summer wind. If the boys couldn't hear the bedsheets flapping on the washline, they could see and feel the autumn day. There were chores and holidays and the wheel of birth and planting, hunting, fishing, and harvest. The boys were familiar in town; nobody ever laughed at them, and when Sarah met neighbors at the store, they praised her sons with exaggerated praise, well meant, saying that no one could tell, no one could really tell unless they knew, about the boys not hearing.

Sarah wanted to cry to these kindly women that the simple orders the boys obeyed by reading her lips were not a miracle. If she could ever hear in their long-practiced robot voices a question that had to do with feelings and not facts, and answer it in words that rose beyond the daily, tangible things done or not done, *that* would be a miracle.

Her neighbors didn't know that they themselves confided to one another from a universe of hopes, a world they wanted half lost in the world that was; how often they spoke pitting inflection against meaning to soften it, harden it, make a joke of it, curse by it, bless by it. They didn't realize how they wrapped the bare words of love in gentle humor or wild insults that the loved ones knew were ways of keeping the secret of love between the speaker and the hearer. Mothers lovingly called their children crow-bait, mouse-meat, devils. They predicted dark ends for them, and the children heard the secrets beneath the words, heard them and smiled and knew, and let the love said-unsaid caress their souls. With her own bitter knowledge Sarah could only thank them for well-meaning and return to silence.

Standing on the back porch now, Sarah heard the wind in the poplars and she sighed. It was getting on to noon. Warm air was beginning to ripple the fields. Matthew would be ready for lunch soon, but she wished she could stand out under the warm sky forever and listen to birds stitching sounds into the endless silence. She found herself thinking about Abel again, and the bride. She wondered what Janice would be like. Abel had gone all the way to Chicago to be trained in drafting. He had met her there, in the school. Sarah was afraid of a girl like that. They had been married quickly, without family or friends or toasts or gifts or questions. It hinted at some kind of secret shame. It frightened her. That kind of girl was independent and she might be scornful of a dowdy mother-in-law. And the house was still a mess.

From down the road, dust was rising. Matthew must have seen it too. He came over the rise and toward the house walking faster than usual. He'd want to slick his hair down and wash up to meet the stranger his son had become. She ran inside and bundled up the unsorted laundry, ran upstairs and pulled a comb through her hair, put on a crooked dab of lipstick, banged her shin, took off her apron and saw a spot on her dress, put the apron on again and shouted a curse to all the disorder she suddenly saw around her.

Now the car was crunching up the thin gravel of the

driveway. She heard Matthew downstairs washing up, not realizing that the bride and groom were already at the house. Protect your own, she thought, and ran down to tell him. Together they went to the door and opened it, hoping that at least Abel's familiar face would comfort them.

They didn't recognize him at first, and he didn't see them. He and the tiny bride might have been alone in the world. He was walking around to open the door for her, helping her out, bringing her up the path to the house, and all the time their fingers and hands moved and spun meanings at which they smiled and laughed; they were talking somehow, painting thoughts in the air so fast with their fingers that Sarah couldn't see where one began and the other ended. She stared. The school people had always told her that such finger-talk set the deaf apart. It was abnormal; it made freaks of them. . . . How soon Abel had accepted someone else's strangeness and bad ways. She felt so dizzy she thought she was going to fall, and she was more bitterly jealous than she had ever been before.

The little bride stopped before them appealingly and in her dead, deaf-rote voice, said, "Ah-am pliizd to meet 'ou." Sarah put out her hand dumbly and it was taken and the girl's eyes shone. Matthew smiled, and this time the girl spoke and waved her hands in time to her words, and then gave Matthew her hand. So Abel had told that girl about Matthew's deafness. It had never been a secret, but Sarah felt somehow betrayed.

They had lunch, saw the farm, the other boys came home from their summer school and met Janice. Sarah put out cake and tea and showed Abel and Janice up to the room she had made ready for them, and all the time the two of them went on with love-talk in their fingers; the jokes and secrets knitted silently between them, fears told and calmed, hopes spoken and echoed in the silence of a kitchen where twenty-five years of silence had imprisoned her. Always they would stop and pull themselves back to their good manners, speaking or writing polite questions and answers for the family; but in a moment or two, the talk would flag, the urgent hunger would overcome them and they would fight it, resolutely turning their eyes to Sarah's mouth. Then the signs would creep into their fingers, and the joy of talk into their faces, and they would fall before the conquering need of their communion.

Sarah's friend Luita came the next day, in the afternoon. They sat over tea with the kitchen window open for the cool breeze and Sarah was relieved and grateful to hold to a familiar thing now that her life had suddenly become so strange to her. Luita hadn't changed at all, thank God—not the hand that waved her tea cool or the high giggle that broke into generous laughter.

"She's darling!" Luita said after Janice had been introduced, and, thankfully, had left them. Sarah didn't want to talk about her, so she agreed without enthusiasm.

Luita only smiled back. "Sarah, you'll never pass for pleased with a face like that."

"It's just—just her ways," Sarah said. "She never even wrote to us before the wedding, and now she comes in and—and changes everything. I'll be honest, Luita, I didn't want Abel to marry someone who was deaf. What did we train him for, all those special classes? . . . *not* to marry another deaf person. And she hangs on him like a wood tick all day . . ." She didn't mention the signs. She couldn't.

Luita said, "It's just somebody new in the house, that's all. She's important to you, but a stranger. Addie Purkhard felt the same way and you know what a lovely girl Velma turned out to be. It just took time. . . . She's going to have a baby, did she tell you?"

"Baby? Who?" Sarah cried, feeling cold and terrified.

"Why, *Velma*. A baby due about a month after my Dolores'."

It had never occurred to Sarah that Janice and Abel could have a baby. She wanted to stop thinking about it and she looked back at Luita whose eyes were glowing with something joyful that had to be said. Luita hadn't been able to see beyond it to the anguish of her friend.

Luita said, "You know, Sarah, things haven't been so good between Sam and me. . . ." She cleared her throat. "You know how stubborn he is. The last few weeks, it's been like a whole new start for us. I came over to tell you about it because I'm so happy, and I had to share it with you."

She looked away shyly, and Sarah pulled herself together and leaned forward, putting her hand on her friend's arm. "I'm so happy for you. What happened?"

"It started about three weeks ago—a night that neither of us could get to sleep. We hadn't been arguing; there was just that awful coldness, as if we'd both been frozen stiff. One of us started talking—just lying there in the dark. I don't even know who started, but pretty soon we were telling each other the most secret things—things we never could have said in the light. He finally told me that Dolores having a baby makes him feel old and scared. He's afraid of it, Sarah, and I never knew it, and it explains why he hates to go over and see them, and why he argues with Ken all the time. Right there beside me he told me so many things I'd forgotten or misunderstood. In the dark it's like thinking out loud—like being alone and yet together at the same time. I love him so and I came so close to forgetting it. . . ."

Sarah lay in bed and thought about Luita and Sam sharing their secrets in the dark. Maybe even now they were talking in their flower-papered upstairs room, moving against the engulfing seas of silence as if in little boats, finding each other and touching and then looking out in awe at the vastness all around them where they might have rowed alone and mute forever. She wondered if Janice and Abel fingered those signs in the dark on each other's body. She began to cry. There was that freedom, at least; other wives had to strangle their weeping.

When she was cried out, she lay in bed and counted all the good things she had: children, possessions, acres of land, respect of neighbors, the years of certainty and success. Then she conjured the little bride, and saw her standing in front of Abel's old car as she had at first—with nothing; all her virtues still unproven, all her fears still forming, and her bed in another woman's house. Against the new gold ring on the bride's finger, Sarah threw all the substance of her years to weigh for her. The balance went with the bride. It wasn't fair! The balance went with the bride because she had put that communion in the scales as well, and all the thoughts that must have been given and taken between them. It outweighed Sarah's twenty-five years of muteness; outweighed the house and barn and well-tended land, and the sleeping family keeping their silent thoughts.

The days went by. Sarah tortured herself with elaborate courtesy to Janice and politeness to the accomplice son, but she couldn't guard her own envy from herself and she found fault wherever she looked. Now the silence of her house was throbbing with her anger. Every morning Janice would come and ask to help, but Sarah was too restless to teach her, so Janice would sit for a while waiting and then get up and go outside to look for Abel. Then Sarah would decide to make coleslaw and sit with the chopping bowl in her lap, smashing the chopper against the wood with a vindictive joy that she alone could hear the sounds she was making, that she alone knew how savage they were and how satisfying.

At church she would see the younger boys all clean and handsome, Matthew greeting friends, Janice demure and fragile, and Abel proud and loving, and she would feel a terrible guilt for her unreasonable anger; but back from town afterwards, and after Sunday dinner, she noticed as never before how disheveled the boys looked, how ugly their hollow voices sounded. Had Matthew always been so patient and unruffled? He was like one of his own stock, an animal, a dumb animal.

Janice kept asking to help and Sarah kept saying there wasn't time to teach her. She was amazed when Matthew, who was very fussy about his fruit, suggested to her that Janice might be able to take care of the grapes and, later, work in the orchard.

"I haven't time to teach her!"

"Ah owill teeech Ja-nuss," Abel said, and they left right after dinner in too much of a hurry.

Matthew stopped Sarah when she was clearing the table and asked why she didn't like Janice. Now it was Sarah's turn to be silent, and when Matthew insisted, Sarah finally turned on him. "You don't understand," she shouted. "You don't understand a thing!" And she saw on his face the same look of confusion she had seen that day in Mama's fussy front room when she had suddenly begun to cry and could not stop. She turned away with the plates, but suddenly his hand shot out and he struck them to the floor, and the voice he couldn't hear or control rose to an awful cry, "Ah ahm dehf! Ah ahm dehf!" Then he went out, slamming the door without the satisfaction of its sound.

If a leaf fell or a stalk sprouted in the grape arbor, Janice told it over like a set of prayers. One night at supper, Sarah saw the younger boys framing those dumb-signs of hers, and she took them outside and slapped their hands. "*We* don't do that!" she shouted at them, and to Janice later she said, "Those . . . signs you make—I know they must have taught you to do that, but out here . . . well, it isn't our way."

Janice looked back at her in a confusion for which there were no words.

It was no use raging at Janice. Before she had come there had never been anything for Sarah to be angry about. . . . What did they all expect of her? Wasn't it enough that she was left out of a world that heard and laughed without being humiliated by the love-madness they made with their hands? It was like watching them undressing.

The wind cannot be caught. Poplars may sift it, a rising bird can breast it, but it will pass by and no one can stop it. She saw the boys coming home at a dead run now, and they couldn't keep their hands from taking letters, words, and pictures from the fingers of the lovers. If they saw an eagle, caught a fish, or got scolded, they ran to their brother or his wife, and Sarah had to stand in the background and demand to be told.

One day Matthew came up to her and smiled and said, "Look." He put out his two index fingers and hooked the right down on the left, then the left down gently on the right. "Fwren," he said, "Ja-nuss say, fwren."

To Sarah there was something obscene about all those gestures, and she said, "I don't like people waving their hands around like monkeys in a zoo!" She said it very clearly so that he couldn't mistake it.

He shook his head violently and gestured as he spoke. "Mouth eat; mouth kiss, mouth tawk! Fin-ger wohk; fin-ger tawk. E-ah" (and he grabbed his ear, violently), "e-ah dehf. *Mihn*," (and he rapped his head, violently, as if turning a terrible impatience against himself so as to spare her) "*mihn not* dehf!"

Later she went to the barn after something and she ran into Lindsay and Franklin Delano standing guiltily, and when she caught them in her eye as she turned, she saw their hands framing signs. They didn't come into the house until it was nearly dark. Was their hunger for those signs so great that only darkness could bring them home? They weren't bad boys, the kind who would do a thing just because you told them not to. Did their days have a hunger too, or was it only the spell of the lovers, honey-honeying to shut out a world of moving mouths and silence?

At supper she looked around the table and was reassured. It could have been any farm family sitting there, respectable and quiet. A glance from the father was all that was needed to keep order or summon another helping. Their eyes were lowered, their faces composed. The hands were quiet. She smiled and went to the kitchen to fix the shortcake she had made as a surprise.

When she came back, they did not notice her immediately. They were all busy talking. Janice was telling them something and they all had their mouths ridiculously pursed with the word. Janice smiled in assent and each one showed her his sign and she smiled at each one and nodded, and the signers turned to one another in their joy, accepting and begging acceptance. Then they saw Sarah standing there; the hands came down, the faces faded.

She took the dinner plates away and brought in the dessert things, and when she went back to the kitchen for the cake, she began to cry. It was beyond envy now; it was too late for measuring or weighing. She had lost. In the country of the blind, Mama used to say, the one-eyed man is king. Having been a citizen of such a country, she knew better. In the country of the deaf, the hearing man is lonely. Into that country a girl had come who, with a wave of her hand, had given the deaf ears for one another, and had made Sarah the deaf one.

Sarah stood, staring at her cake and feeling for that moment the profundity of the silence which she had once tried to match by stuffing cotton in her ears. Everyone she loved was in the other room, talking, sharing, standing before the awful, impersonal heaven and the unhearing earth with pictures of his thoughts, and she was the deaf one now. It wasn't "any farm family," silent in its strength. It was a yearning family, silent in its hunger, and a demure little bride had shown them all how deep the hunger was. She had shown Sarah that her youth had been sold into silence. She was too old to change now.

An anger rose in her as she stared at the cake. Why should they be free to move and gesture and look different while she was kept in bondage to their silence? Then she remembered Matthew's mute notes, his pride in Abel's training, his face when he had cried, "I am deaf!" over and over. She had actually fought that terrible yearning, that hunger they all must have had for their own words. If they could all speak somehow, what would the boys tell her?

She knew what she wanted to tell them. That the wind sounds through the poplar trees, and people have a hard time speaking to one another even if they aren't deaf. Luita and Sam had to have a night to hide their faces while they spoke. It suddenly occurred to her that if Matthew made one of those signs with his hands and she could learn that sign, she could put her hands against his in the darkness, and read the meaning—that if she learned those signs she could hear him. . . .

She dried her eyes hurriedly and took in the cake. They saw her and the hands stopped, drooping lifelessly again; the faces waited mutely. Silence. It was a silence she could no longer bear. She looked from face to face. What was behind those eyes she loved? Didn't everyone's world go deeper than chores and bread and sleep?

"I want to talk to you," she said. "I want to talk, to know what you think." She put her hands out before her, offering them.

Six pairs of eyes watched her.

Janice said, "Mo-ther."

Eyes snapped away to Janice; thumb was under lip: the Sign.

Sarah followed them. "Wife," she said, showing her ring.

"Wife," Janice echoed, thumb under lip to the clasp of hands.

Sarah said, "I love. . . ."

Janice showed her and she followed hesitantly and then turned to Matthew to give and to be received in that sign.

The Game

by Judith Ortiz Cofer

*As you read this poem, consider what
similarities there might be between those
sharing Cruz's world and those who share
Helen Keller's.*

The little humpbacked girl
did not go to school,
but was kept home to help her mother,
an unsmiling woman with other children
5   whose spines were not twisted
into the symbol of a family's shame.

At birth,
on first seeing the child
curled into a question mark,
10   the eternal *why*
she would have to carry home,
she gave her the name of Cruz,
for the cross Christ bore
to Calvary.

15   In my house,
we did not speak of her affliction,
but acted as if Cruz,
whose lovely head
sat incongruously upon a body
20   made of stuck-together parts—
like a child's first attempt
at cutting and pasting a paper doll—
was the same
as any of my other friends.

25   But when she stood at our door,
waiting for me to go out and play,
Mother fell silent, awed, perhaps,
by the sight
of one of her God's small mysteries.

30   Running to her backyard,
Cruz and I would enter a playhouse
she had built of palm fronds
where we'd play her favorite game: "family."
I was always cast in the role
35   of husband or child—perfect
in my parts—I'd praise her lavishly
for the imaginary dishes
she placed before me,
while she laughed, delighted
40   at my inventions, lost in the game,
until it started getting too late
to play pretend.

Miss Awful

by Arthur Cavanaugh

*At one point, Annie Sullivan says to
Dr. Anagnos, "The only time I have trouble
is when I'm right. Is it my fault it's so
often?" It's possible that Miss Orville,
the teacher portrayed in this story, would
make a similar statement about her
own life.*

The whole episode of Miss Awful began for the Clarks
at their dinner table one Sunday afternoon. Young
Roger Clark was explaining why he could go to
Central Park with his father instead of staying home
to finish his homework—Miss Wilson, his teacher,
wouldn't be at school tomorrow, so who'd know the
difference? "She has to take care of a crisis," Roger
explained. "It's in Omaha."

"What is?" his older sister, Elizabeth, inquired.
"For a kid in third grade, Roger, you talk dopey. You
fail to make sense."

Roger ignored the insult. His sister was a condition
of life he had learned to live with, like lions. Or
snakes. Poisonous ones. Teetering, as always, on the
tilted-back chair, feet wrapped around the legs, he
continued, "Till Miss Wilson gets back, we're having
some other teacher. She flew to Omaha yesterday." He
pushed some peas around on his plate and was silent
a moment. "I hope her plane don't crash," he said.

Roger's mother patted his hand. A lively, outgoing
youngster, as noisy and rambunctious as any seven-
year-old, he had another side to him, tender and soft,
which worried about people. Let the blind man who

sold pencils outside the five-and-ten on Broadway be absent from his post, and Roger worried that catastrophe had overtaken him. When Mrs. Loomis, a neighbor of the Clarks in the Greenwich Village brownstone, had entered the hospital, Roger's anxious queries had not ceased until she was discharged. And recently there was the cat, which had nested in the downstairs doorway at night. Roger had carried down saucers of milk, clucking with concern. "Is the cat run away? Don't it have a home?"

Virginia Clark assured her son, "You'll have Miss Wilson safely back before you know it. It's nice that you care so."

Roger beamed with relief. "Well, I like Miss Wilson; she's fun. Last week, for instance, when Tommy Miller got tired of staying in his seat and lay down on the floor—"

"He did what?" Roger's father was roused from his postdinner torpor.

"Sure. Pretty soon the whole class was lying down. Know what Miss Wilson did?"

"If you'll notice, Mother," Elizabeth interjected, "he hasn't touched a single pea."

"*She* lay down on the floor, too," Roger went on ecstatically. "She said we'd *all* have a rest. It was perfectly normal in the middle of the day. That's what I love about St. Geoff's. It's fun."

"Fun," snorted his sister. "School isn't supposed to be a fun fest. It's supposed to be filling that empty noodle of yours."

"Miss Wilson got down on the floor?" Mr. Clark repeated. He had met Roger's teacher on occasion; she had struck him as capable but excessively whimsical. She was a large woman to be getting down on floors, Mr. Clark thought. "What did the class do next?" he asked.

"Oh, we lay there a while, then got up and did a

Mexican hat dance," Roger answered. "It was swell."

"I'm sure not every day is as frolicsome," Mrs. Clark countered, slightly anxious. She brought in dessert, a chocolate mousse. Roger's story sounded typical of St. Geoffrey's. Not that she was unhappy with his school. A small private institution, while it might be called overly permissive, it projected a warm, homey atmosphere which Mrs. Clark found appealing. It was church affiliated, which she approved of, and heaven knows its location a few blocks away from the brownstone was convenient. True, Roger's scholastic progress wasn't notable—his spelling, for example, remained atrocious. Friendly as St. Geoffrey's was, Mrs. Clark sometimes *did* wish . . .

Roger attacked dessert with a lot more zest than he had shown the peas. "So can I go to the park with you, Dad? I've only got spelling left, and who cares about that?" Before his mother could comment, he was up from the table and racing toward the coat closet. "OK, Dad?"

"I didn't say you could go. I didn't even say I'd take you," Mr. Clark objected. He happened, at that moment, to glance at his waistline and reflect that a brisk hike might do him some good. He pushed back his chair. "All right, but the minute we return, it's straight to your room to finish your spelling."

"Ah, thanks, Dad. Can we go to the boat pond first?"

"We will not," cried Elizabeth, elbowing into the closet. "We'll go to the Sheep Meadow first."

Roger was too happy to argue. Pulling on his jacket, he remarked, "Gee, I wonder what the new teacher will be like. Ready for your coat, Dad?"

It was just as well that he gave the matter no more thought. In view of events to come, Roger was entitled to a few carefree hours.

Monday morning at school started off with perfect normalcy. It began exactly like any other school morning. Elizabeth had long since departed for the girls' school she attended uptown when Mrs. Clark set out with Roger for the short walk to St. Geoff's. She didn't trust him with the Fifth Avenue traffic yet. They reached the school corner, and Roger skipped away eagerly from her. The sidewalk in front of school already boasted a large, jostling throng of children, and his legs couldn't hurry Roger fast enough to join them. Indeed, it was his reason for getting to school promptly: to have time to play before the 8:45 bell. Roger's school bag was well equipped for play. As usual, he'd packed a supply of baseball cards for trading opportunities; a spool of string, in case anybody brought a kite; a water pistol for possible use in the lavatory; and a police whistle for sheer noise value. Down the Greenwich Village sidewalk he galloped, shouting the names of his third-grade friends as he picked out faces from the throng. "Hiya, Tommy. Hey, hiya, Bruce. Hi, Steve, you bring your trading cards?"

By the time the 8:45 bell rang—St. Geoff's used a cowbell, one of the homey touches—Roger had finished a game of tag, traded several baseball cards, and was launched in an exciting jump-the-hydrant contest. Miss Gillis, the school secretary, was in charge of the bell, and she had to clang it extensively before the student body took notice. Clomping up the front steps, they spilled into the downstairs hall, headed in various directions. Roger's class swarmed up the stairs in rollicking spirits—Tommy Miller, Bruce Reeves, Joey Lambert, with the girls forming an untidy rear flank behind them, shrill with laughter.

It wasn't until the front ranks reached the third-grade classroom that the first ominous note was struck.

"Hey, what's going on?" Jimmy Moore demanded, first to observe the changed appearance of the room. The other children crowded behind him in the doorway. Instead of a cozy semicircle—"As though we're seated around a glowing hearth," Miss Wilson had described it—the desks and chairs had been rearranged in stiff, rigid rows. "Gee, look, the desks are in rows," commented Midge Fuller, a plump little girl who stood blocking Roger's view. Midge was a child given to unnecessary statements. "It's raining today," she would volunteer to her classmates, all of them shod in slickers and rubbers. Or, "There's the lunch bell, gang." The point to Roger wasn't that the desks had been rearranged. The point was, *why?* As if in answer, he heard two hands clap behind him as loud and menacing as thunder.

"What's this, what's this?" barked a stern, raspish voice. "You are not cattle milling in a pen. Enough foolish gaping! Come, come, form into lines."

Heads turned in unison, mouths fell agape. The children of St. Geoffrey's third grade had never formed into lines of any sort, but this was not the cause of their shocked inertia. Each was staring, with a sensation similar to that of drowning, at the owner of the raspish voice. She was tall and straight as a ruler and was garbed in an ancient tweed suit whose skirt dipped nearly to the ankles. She bore a potted plant in one arm and Miss Wilson's roll book in the other. Rimless spectacles glinted on her bony nose. Her hair was gray, like a witch's, skewered in a bun, and there was no question that she had witch's eyes. Roger had seen those same eyes leering from the pages of *Hansel and Gretel*—identical, they were. He gulped at the terrible presence.

"Are you a class of deaf mutes?" he heard with a start. "Form lines, I said. Girls in one, boys in the other." Poking, prodding, patrolling back and forth, the new teacher kneaded the third grade into position and ruefully inspected the result. "Sloppiest group I've ever beheld. *March!*" She clapped time with her hands, and the stunned ranks trooped into the classroom. "*One,* two, three, *one,* two—girls on the window side, boys on the wall. Stand at your desks. Remove your outer garments. You, little miss, with the vacant stare. What's your name?"

"Ja-ja—" a voice squeaked.

"Speak up. I won't have mumblers."

"Jane Douglas."

"Well, Jane Douglas, you will be coat monitor. Collect the garments a row at a time and hang them neatly in the cloakroom. Did you hear me, child? Stop staring." Normally slow-moving, Jane Douglas became a whirl of activity, charging up and down the aisles, piling coats in her arms. The new teacher tugged at her tweed jacket. "Class be seated, hands folded on desks," she barked, and there was immediate compliance. She next paraded to the windows and installed the potted plant on the sill. Her witch's hands fussed with the green leaves, straightening, pruning. "Plants and children belong in classrooms," she declared, spectacles sweeping over the rows. "Can someone suggest why?"

There was total silence, punctured by a deranged giggle, quickly suppressed.

"Very well, I will tell you. Plants and children are living organisms. Both will grow with proper care. Repeat, *proper.* Not indulgent fawning or giving in to whims—scrupulosity!" With another tug at the jacket, she strode, ruler straight, to the desk in the front of the room. "I am Miss Orville. O-r-v-i-l-l-e," she spelled. "You are to use my name in replying to all questions."

In the back of the room, Jimmy Moore whispered

frantically to Roger. "What did she say her name is?"

Miss Orville rapped her desk. "Attention, please, no muttering in the back." She cleared her voice and resumed. "Prior to my retirement I taught boys and girls for forty-six years," she warned. "I am beyond trickery, so I advise you to try none. You are to be in my charge until the return of Miss Wilson, however long that may be." She clasped her hands in front of her and trained her full scrutiny on the rows. "Since I have no knowledge of your individual abilities, perhaps a look at the weekend homework will shed some light. Miss Wilson left me a copy of the assignment. You have all completed it, I trust? Take out your notebooks, please. At once, at once, I say."

Roger's head spun dizzily around. He gaped at the monstrous tweed figure in dismay. Book bags were being clicked open, notebooks drawn out—what was he to do? He had gone to his room after the outing in the park yesterday, but alas, it had not been to complete his assignment. He watched, horrified, as the tweed figure proceeded among the aisles and inspected notebooks. What had she said her name was? Awful—was that it? Miss Awful! Biting his lip, he listened to her scathing comments.

"You call this chicken scrawl penmanship?" R-r-rip! A page was torn out and thrust at its owner. "Redo it at once; it assaults the intelligence." Then, moving on, "What is this maze of ill-spelled words? Not a composition, I trust."

Ill-spelled words! He was in for it for sure. The tweed figure was heading down his aisle. She was three desks away, no escaping it. Roger opened his book bag. It slid from his grasp and, with a crash, fell to the floor. Books, pencil case spilled out. Baseball cards scattered, the water pistol, the police whistle, the spool of string . . .

"Ah," crowed Miss Awful, instantly at his desk, scooping up the offending objects. "We have come to play, have we?"

And she fixed her witch's gaze on him.

Long before the week's end, it was apparent to Virginia Clark that something was drastically wrong with her son's behavior. The happy-go-lucky youngster had disappeared, as if down a well. Another creature had replaced him, nervous, harried, continuously glancing over his shoulder in the manner of one being followed. Mrs. Clark's first inkling of change occurred that same Monday. She had been chatting with the other mothers who congregated outside St. Geoffrey's at three every afternoon to pick up their offspring. A casual assembly, the mothers were as relaxed and informal as the school itself, lounging against the picket fence, exchanging small talk and anecdotes.

"That darling cowbell," laughed one of the group at the familiar clang. "Did I tell you Anne's class is having a taffy pull on Friday? Where else, in the frantic city of New York . . ."

The third grade was the last class to exit from the building on Monday. Not only that, but Mrs. Clark noted that the children appeared strangely subdued. Some of them were actually reeling, all but dazed. As for Roger, eyes taut and pleading, he quickly pulled his mother down the block, signaling for silence. When enough distance had been gained, words erupted from him.

"No, we don't have a new teacher," he flared wildly. "We got a *witch* for a new teacher. It's the truth. She's from *Hansel and Gretel,* the same horrible eyes—and she steals toys. *Yes,*" he repeated in mixed outrage and hurt. "By accident you happen to put some toys in your book bag, and she *steals* 'em. I'll fool her! I won't *bring* any more toys to school," he howled. "Know what children are to her? Plants! She did, she called us plants. Miss Awful, that's her name."

Such was Roger's distress that his mother offered to stop at the Schrafft's on Thirteenth Street and treat him to a soda. "Who's got time for sodas?" he bleated. "I have homework to do. Punishment homework. Ten words, ten times each. On account of the witch's spelling test."

"Ten words, ten times each?" Mrs. Clark repeated. "How many words were on the test?"

"Ten," moaned Roger. "Every one wrong. Come on. I've got to hurry home. I don't have time to waste." Refusing to be consoled, he headed for the brownstone and the desk in his room.

On Tuesday, together with the other mothers, Mrs. Clark was astonished to see the third grade march down the steps of St. Geoffrey's in military precision. Clop, clop, the children marched, looking neither to the left nor right, while behind them came a stiff-backed, iron-haired woman in a pepper-and-salt suit. "*One,* two, three, *one,* two, three," she counted, then clapped her hands in dismissal. Turning, she surveyed the assemblage of goggle-eyed mothers. "May I inquire if the mother of Joseph Lambert is among you?" she asked.

"I'm Mrs. Lambert," replied a voice meekly, whereupon Miss Orville paraded directly up to her. The rest of the mothers looked on, speechless.

"Mrs. Lambert, your son threatens to grow into a useless member of society," stated Miss Orville in ringing tones that echoed down the street. "That is, unless you term watching television useful. Joseph has confessed that he views three hours per evening."

"Only after his homework's finished," Margery Lambert allowed.

"Madame, he does not finish his homework. He idles through it, scattering mistakes higgledy-piggledy. I suggest you give him closer supervision. Good day." With a brief nod, Miss Orville proceeded down the street, and it was a full minute before the mothers had recovered enough to comment. Some voted in favor of immediate protest to Dr. Jameson, St. Geoffrey's headmaster, on the hiring of such a woman, even on a temporary basis. But since it was temporary, the mothers concluded it would have to be tolerated.

Nancy Reeves, Bruce's mother, kept staring at the retreating figure of Miss Orville, by now far down the block. "I know her from somewhere, I'm sure of it," she insisted, shaking her head.

The next morning, Roger refused to leave for school. "My shoes aren't shined," he wailed. "Not what Miss Awful calls shined. Where's the polish? I can't leave till I do 'em over."

"Roger, if only you'd thought of it last night," sighed Mrs. Clark.

"You sound like her," he cried. "That's what *she'd* say," and it gave his mother something to puzzle over for the rest of the day. She was still thinking about it when she joined the group of mothers outside St. Geoffrey's at three. She had to admit it was sort of impressive, the smart, martial air exhibited by the third grade as they trooped down the steps. There was to be additional ceremony today. The ranks waited on the sidewalk until Miss Orville passed back and forth in inspection. Stationing herself at the head of the columns, she boomed, "Good afternoon, boys and girls. Let us return with perfect papers tomorrow."

"Good aaaaafternoon, Miss Orville," the class sang back in unison, after which the ranks broke. Taking little Amy Lewis in tow, Miss Orville once more nodded at the mothers. "Which is she?" she asked Amy.

Miss Orville approached the trapped Mrs. Lewis. She cleared her throat, thrust back her shoulders. "Amy tells me she is fortunate enough to enjoy the services of a full-time domestic at home," said Miss Orville. "May I question whether she is fortunate—or deprived? I needn't lecture you, I'm sure, Mrs. Lewis, about the wisdom of assigning a child tasks to perform at home. Setting the table, tidying up one's room, are lessons in self-reliance for the future. Surely you agree." There was a nod from Mrs. Lewis. "Excellent," smiled Miss Orville. "Amy will inform me in the morning the tasks you have assigned her. Make them plentiful, I urge you."

The lecturing, however, was not ended. Turning from Mrs. Lewis, Miss Orville cast her gaze around and inquired, "Is Roger Clark's mother present?"

"Yes?" spoke Virginia Clark, reaching for Roger's hand. "What is it?"

Miss Orville studied Roger silently for a long moment. "A scallywag, if ever I met one," she pronounced. The rimless spectacles lifted to the scallywag's mother. "You know, of course, that Roger is a prodigy," said Miss Orville. "A prodigy of misspelling. Roger, spell *flower* for us," she ordered. "Come, come, speak up."

Roger kept his head lowered. "F," he spelled. "F-l-o-r."

"Spell *castle*."

"K," spelled Roger. "K-a-z-l."

Miss Orville's lips parted grimly. "Those are the results, mind you, of an hour's solid work with your son, Mrs. Clark. He does not apply himself. He wishes to remain a child at play, absorbed in his toys. Is that what you want for him?"

"I—I—" Virginia Clark would have been grateful if the sidewalk had opened up to receive her.

As she reported to her husband that evening, she had never in her life been as mortified. "Spoke to me in front of all the other mothers in loud, clarion tones," she described the scene. "Do I want Roger to remain a child at play. Imagine."

"By the way, where is Roge?" Mr. Clark asked, who had come home late from the office. "He's not watching television or busy with his airplanes—"

"In his room, doing over his homework for the ninety-eighth time. It has to be perfect, he says. But really, Charles, don't you think it was outrageous?"

Mr. Clark stirred his coffee. "I bet Miss Orville doesn't get down on the floor with the class. Or do Mexican hat dances with them."

"If that's meant to disparage Miss Wilson—" Virginia Clark stacked the dinner dishes irritably. She sometimes found her husband's behavior maddening. Especially when he took to grinning at her, as he was presently doing. She also concluded that she'd had her fill of Elizabeth's attitude on the subject. "At least some teacher's wised up to Roge," had been the Clarks' daughter's comment. "He's cute and all, but I wouldn't want to be in a shipwreck with him." Washing dishes in the kitchen, Mrs. Clark considered that maybe she wouldn't meet Roger in *front* of school tomorrow. Maybe she'd wait at the corner instead. "His shoes," she gasped, and hurried to remind her son to get out the polishing kit. The spelling, too, she'd better work on that . . .

It was on Thursday that Nancy Reeves finally remembered where, previously, she had seen Miss Orville. Perhaps it was from the shock of having received a compliment from the latter.

"Mrs. Reeves, I rejoice to inform you of progress," Miss Orville had addressed her after the third grade had performed its military display for the afternoon. "On Monday, young Bruce's penmanship was comparable to a chicken's—if a chicken could write. Today, I was pleased to award him an A."

A tug at the tweed jacket, and the stiff-backed figure walked firmly down the street. Nancy Reeves stared after her until Miss Orville had merged into the flow of pedestrians and traffic. "I know who she is," Nancy suddenly remarked, turning to the other mothers. "I knew I'd seen her before. Those old ramshackle buildings near us on Hudson Street—remember when they were torn down last year?" The other mothers formed a circle around her. "Miss Orville was one of the tenants," Nancy Reeves went on. "She'd lived there for ages and refused to budge until the landlord got a court order and deposited her on the sidewalk. I *saw* her there, sitting in a rocker on the sidewalk surrounded by all this furniture and plants. Her picture was in the papers. Elderly retired schoolteacher . . . they found a furnished room for her on Jane Street, I think. Poor old thing, evicted like that . . . I remember she couldn't keep any of the plants . . ."

On the way home, after supplying a lurid account of the day's tortures—"Miss Awful made Walter Meade stand in the corner for saying a bad word"—Roger asked his mother, "Eviction. What does that mean?"

"It's when somebody is forced by law to vacate an apartment. The landlord gets an eviction notice, and the person has to leave."

"Kicked her out on the street. Is that what they did to the witch?"

"Don't call her that; it's rude and impolite," Mrs. Clark said as they turned into the brownstone doorway. "I can see your father and I have been too easygoing where you're concerned."

"Huh, we've got worse names for her," Roger

retorted. "*Curse* names; you should hear 'em. We're planning how to get even with Miss Awful, just you see." He paused as his mother opened the downstairs door with her key. "That's where the cat used to sleep, remember?" he said, pointing at a corner of the entryway. His face was grave and earnest. "I wonder where that cat went to. Hey, Mom," he hurried to catch up. "Maybe *it* was evicted, too."

Then it was Friday at St. Geoffrey's. Before lunch, Miss Orville told the class, "I am happy to inform you that Miss Wilson will be back on Monday." She held up her hand for quiet. "This afternoon will be my final session with you. Not that discipline will relax, but I might read you a story. Robert Louis Stevenson, perhaps. My boys and girls always enjoyed him so. Forty-six years of them . . . Joseph Lambert, you're not sitting up straight. You know I don't permit slouchers in my class."

It was a mistake to have told the class that Miss Wilson would be back on Monday, that only a few hours of the terrible reign of Miss Awful were left to endure. Even before lunch recess, a certain spirit of challenge and defiance had infiltrated into the room. Postures were still erect but not quite as erect. Tommy Miller dropped his pencil case on the floor and did not request permission to pick it up.

"Ahhh, so what," he mumbled when Miss Orville remonstrated with him.

"What did you say?" she demanded, drawing herself up.

"I said, so what," Tommy Miller answered, returning her stare without distress.

Roger thought that was neat of Tommy, talking fresh like that. He was surprised, too, because Miss Awful didn't yell at Tommy or anything. A funny look came into her eyes, he noticed, and she just went on with the geography lesson. And when Tommy dropped his pencil case again and picked it up without asking, she said nothing. Roger wasn't so certain that Tommy should have dropped the pencil case a second time. The lunch bell rang then, and he piled out of the classroom with the others, not bothering to wait for permission.

At lunch in the basement cafeteria, the third grade talked of nothing except how to get even with Miss Awful. The recommendations showed daring and imagination.

"We could beat her up," Joey Lambert suggested. "We could wait at the corner till she goes by and throw rocks at her."

"We'd get arrested," Walter Meade pointed out.

"Better idea," said Bruce Reeves. "We could go upstairs to the classroom before she gets back and tie a string in front of the door. She'd trip and break her neck."

"She's old," Roger Clark protested. "We can't hurt her like that. She's too old."

It was one of the girls, actually, who thought of the plant. "That dopey old plant she's always fussing over," piped Midge Fuller. "We could rip off all the dopey leaves. That'd show her."

Roger pushed back his chair and stood up from the table. "We don't want to do that," he said, not understanding why he objected. It was a feeling inside he couldn't explain . . . "Aw, let's forget about it," he said. "Let's call it quits."

"The plant, the plant," Midge Fuller squealed, clapping her hands.

Postures were a good deal worse when the third grade reconvened after lunch. "Well, you've put in an industrious week, I dare say . . . ," Miss Orville commented. She opened the frayed volume of *Treasure Island* which she had brought from home and turned the pages carefully to Chapter One. "I assume the class is familiar with the tale of young Jim Hawkins, Long John Silver, and the other wonderful characters."

"No, I ain't," said Tommy Miller.

"Ain't. What word is that?"

"It's the word *ain't*," answered Tommy.

"Ain't, ain't," somebody jeered.

Miss Orville lowered the frayed volume. "No, children, you mustn't do this," she said with force. "To attend school is a privilege you must not mock. Can you guess how many thousands of children in the world are denied the gift of schooling?" Her lips quavered. "It is a priceless gift. You cannot permit yourselves to squander a moment of it." She rose from her desk and looked down at the rows of boys and girls. "It isn't enough any longer to accept a gift and make no return for it, not with the world in the shape it's in," she said, spectacles trembling on her bony nose. "The world isn't a play box," she said. "If I have been severe with you this past week, it was for your benefit. The world needs good citizens. If I have helped one of you to grow a fraction of an inch, if just *one* of you—"

She stopped speaking. Her voice faltered, the words dammed up. She was staring at the plant on the windowsill, which she had not noticed before. The stalks twisted up bare and naked where the leaves had been torn off. "You see," Miss Orville said after a moment, going slowly to the windowsill. "You *see* what I am talking about? To be truly educated is to be civilized. Here, you may observe the opposite." Her fingers reached out to the bare stalks. "Violence and destruction . . ." She turned and faced the class, and behind the spectacles her eyes were dim and faded. "Whoever is responsible, I beg of you only to be sorry," she said. When she returned to her desk, her back was straighter than ever, but it seemed to take her longer to cover the distance.

At the close of class that afternoon, there was no forming of lines. Miss Orville merely dismissed the boys and girls and did not leave her desk. The children ran out, some in regret, some silent, others cheerful and scampering. Only Roger Clark stayed behind.

He stood at the windows, plucking at the naked plant on the sill. Miss Orville was emptying the desk of her possessions, books, pads, a folder of maps. "These are yours, I believe," she said to Roger. In her hands were the water pistol, the baseball cards, the spool of string. "Here, take them," she said.

Roger went to the desk. He stuffed the toys in his coat pocket without paying attention to them. He stood at the desk, rubbing his hand up and down his coat.

"Yes?" Miss Orville asked.

Roger stood back, hands at his side, and lifted his head erectly. "Flower," he spelled. "F-l-o-w-e-r." He squared his shoulders and looked at Miss Orville's brimming eyes. "Castle," Roger spelled. "C-a-s-t-l-e."

Then he walked from the room.

A Man

by Nina Cassian
translated by Roy MacGregor-Hastie

*Annie Sullivan's conflict with members
of the Keller family centers around their
tendency to pity Helen. This poem also
deals with the temptation of pity.*

While fighting for his country, he lost an arm
and was suddenly afraid:
"From now on, I shall only be able to do
   things by halves.
I shall reap half a harvest.
5   I shall be able to play either the tune
or the accompaniment on the piano,
but never both parts together.
I shall be able to bang with only one fist
on doors, and worst of all
10   I shall only be able to half hold
my love close to me.
There will be things I cannot do at all,
applaud for example,
at shows where everyone applauds."

15   From that moment on, he set himself to do
   everything with twice as much enthusiasm.
And where the arm had been torn away
a wing grew.

from Seeing

by Annie Dillard

Helen Keller remained blind throughout her life, yet she had a deep appreciation of nature. This essay is the work of an author known for her highly developed powers of observation. Reading it may cause you to think not only about your own ability to see but your ability to appreciate.

When I was six or seven years old, growing up in Pittsburgh, I used to take a precious penny of my own and hide it for someone else to find. It was a curious compulsion; sadly, I've never been seized by it since. For some reason I always "hid" the penny along the same stretch of sidewalk up the street. I would cradle it at the roots of a sycamore, say, or in a hole left by a chipped-off piece of sidewalk. Then I would take a piece of chalk, and, starting at either end of the block, draw huge arrows leading up to the penny from both directions. After I learned to write I labeled the arrows: SURPRISE AHEAD or MONEY THIS WAY. I was greatly excited, during all this arrow-drawing, at the thought of the first lucky passer-by who would receive in this way, regardless of merit, a free gift from the universe. But I never lurked about. I would go straight home and not give the matter another thought, until, some months later, I would be gripped again by the impulse to hide another penny.

It is still the first week in January, and I've got great plans. I've been thinking about seeing. There are lots of things to see, unwrapped gifts and free surprises. The world is fairly studded and strewn with pennies cast broadside from a generous hand. But—and this is the point—who gets excited by a mere penny? If you follow one arrow, if you crouch motionless on a bank to watch a tremulous ripple thrill on the water and are rewarded by the sight of a muskrat kit paddling from its den, will you count that sight a chip of copper only, and go your rueful way? It is dire poverty indeed when a man is so malnourished and fatigued that he won't stoop to pick up a penny. But if you cultivate a healthy poverty and simplicity, so that finding a penny will literally make your day, then, since the world is in fact planted in pennies, you have with your poverty bought a lifetime of days. It is that simple. What you see is what you get. . . .

Unfortunately, nature is very much a now-you-see-it, now-you-don't affair. A fish flashes, then dissolves in the water before my eyes like so much salt. Deer apparently ascend bodily into heaven; the brightest oriole fades into leaves. These disappearances stun me into stillness and concentration; they say of nature that it conceals with a grand nonchalance, and they say of vision that it is a deliberate gift, the revelation of a dancer who for my eyes only flings away her seven veils. For nature does reveal as well as conceal: now-you-don't-see-it, now-you-do. For a week last September migrating red-winged blackbirds were feeding heavily down by the creek at the back of the house. One day I went out to investigate the racket; I walked up to a tree, an Osage orange, and a hundred birds flew away. They simply materialized out of the tree. I saw a tree, then a whisk of color, then a tree again. I walked closer and another hundred blackbirds took flight. Not a branch, not a twig budged: the birds were apparently weightless as well as invisible. Or, it was as if the leaves of the Osage orange had been freed from a spell in the form of red-winged blackbirds; they flew from the tree, caught my eye in the sky, and vanished. When I looked again at the tree the leaves had reassembled as if nothing had happened. Finally I walked directly to the trunk of the tree and a final hundred, the real diehards, appeared, spread, and vanished. How could so many hide in the tree without my seeing them? The Osage orange, unruffled, looked just as it had looked from the house, when three hundred red-winged blackbirds cried from its crown. I looked downstream where they flew, and they were gone. Searching, I couldn't spot one. I wandered downstream to force them to play their hand, but they'd crossed the creek and scattered. One show to a customer. These appearances catch at my throat; they are the free gifts, the bright coppers at the roots of trees. . . .

Darkness appalls and light dazzles; the scrap of visible light that doesn't hurt my eyes hurts my brain. What I see sets me swaying. Size and distance and the sudden swelling of meanings confuse me, bowl me over. I straddle the sycamore log bridge over Tinker Creek in the summer. I look at the lighted creek bottom: snail tracks tunnel the mud in quavering curves. A crayfish jerks, but by the time I absorb what has happened, he's gone in a billowing smokescreen of silt. I look at the water: minnows and shiners. If I'm thinking minnows, a carp will fill my brain till I scream. I look at the water's surface: skaters, bubbles, and leaves sliding down. Suddenly, my own face, reflected, startles me witless. Those snails have been tracking my face! Finally, with a shuddering wrench of the will, I see clouds, cirrus clouds. I'm dizzy, I fall in. This looking business is risky.

Once I stood on a humped rock on nearby Purgatory Mountain, watching through binoculars the great autumn hawk migration below, until I discovered that I was in danger of joining the hawks on a vertical migration of my own. I was used to binoculars, but not, apparently, to balancing on humped rocks while looking through them. I staggered. Everything advanced and receded by turns; the world was full of unexplained foreshortenings and depths. A distant huge tan object, a hawk the size of an elephant, turned out to be the browned bough of a nearby loblolly pine. I followed a sharp-shinned hawk against a featureless sky, rotating my head unawares as it flew, and when I lowered the glass a glimpse of my own looming shoulder sent me staggering. What prevents the men on Palomar from falling, voiceless and blinded, from their tiny, vaulted chairs? . . .

I chanced on a wonderful book by Marius von Senden, called *Space and Sight*. When Western surgeons discovered how to perform safe cataract operations, they ranged across Europe and America operating on dozens of men and women of all ages who had been blinded by cataracts since birth. Von Senden collected accounts of such cases; the histories are fascinating. Many doctors had tested their patients' sense perceptions and ideas of space both before and after the operations. The vast majority of patients, of both sexes and all ages, had, in von Senden's opinion, no idea of space whatsoever. Form, distance, and size were so many meaningless syllables. A patient "had no idea of depth, confusing it with roundness." Before the operation a doctor would give a blind patient a cube and a sphere; the patient would tongue it or feel it with his hands, and name it correctly. After the operation the doctor would show the same objects to the patient without letting him touch them; now he had no clue whatsoever what he was seeing. One patient called lemonade "square" because it pricked on his tongue as a square shape pricked on the touch of his hands. Of another postoperative patient, the doctor writes, "I have found in her no notion of size, for example, not even within the narrow limits which she might have encompassed with the aid of touch. Thus when I asked her to show me how big her mother was, she did not stretch out her hands, but set her two index fingers a few inches apart." Other doctors reported their patients' own statements to similar effect. "The room he was in . . . he knew to be but part of the house, yet he could not conceive that the whole house could look bigger"; "Those who are blind from birth . . . have no real conception of height or distance. A house that is a mile away is thought of as nearby, but requiring the taking of a lot of steps. . . . The elevator that whizzes him up and down gives no more sense of vertical distance than does the train of horizontal."

For the newly sighted, vision is pure sensation unencumbered by meaning: "The girl went through the experience that we all go through and forget, the moment we are born. She saw, but it did not mean anything but a lot of different kinds of brightness." Again, "I asked the patient what he could see; he answered that he saw an extensive field of light, in which everything appeared dull, confused, and in motion. He could not distinguish objects." Another patient saw "nothing but a confusion of forms and colours." When a newly sighted girl saw photographs and paintings, she asked, "'Why do they put those dark marks all over them?' 'Those aren't dark marks,' her mother explained, 'those are shadows. That is one of the ways the eye knows that things have shape. If it were not for shadows many things would look flat.' 'Well, that's how things do look,' Joan answered. 'Everything looks flat with dark patches.'"

But it is the patients' concepts of space that are most revealing. One patient, according to his doctor, "practiced his vision in a strange fashion; thus he takes off one of his boots, throws it some way off in front of him, and then attempts to gauge the distance at which it lies; he takes a few steps towards the boot and tries to grasp it; on failing to reach it, he moves on a step or two and gropes for the boot until he finally gets hold of it." "But even at this stage, after three weeks' experience of seeing," von Senden goes on, "'space,' as he conceives it, ends with visual space, i.e. with colour-patches that happen to bound his view. He does not yet have the notion that a larger object (a chair) can mask a smaller one (a dog), or that the latter can still be present even though it is not directly seen."

In general the newly sighted see the world as a dazzle of color-patches. They are pleased by the sensation of color, and learn quickly to name the colors, but the rest of seeing is tormentingly difficult. Soon after his operation a patient "generally bumps into one of these colour-patches and observes them to be substantial, since they resist him as tactual objects do. In walking about it also strikes him—or can if he pays attention—that he is continually passing in between the colours he sees, that he can go past a visual object, that a part of it then steadily disappears from view; and that in spite of this, however he twists and turns—whether entering the room from the door, for example, or returning back to it—he always has a visual space in front of him. Thus he gradually comes to realize that there is also a space behind him, which he does not see."

The mental effort involved in these reasonings proves overwhelming for many patients. It oppresses them to realize, if they ever do at all, the tremendous size of the world, which they had previously conceived of as something touchingly manageable. It oppresses them to realize that they have been visible to people all along, perhaps unattractively so, without their knowledge or consent. A disheartening number of them refuse to use their new vision, continuing to go over objects with their tongues, and lapsing into apathy and despair. "The child can see, but will not make use of his sight. Only when pressed can he with difficulty be brought to look at objects in his neighbourhood; but more than a foot away it is impossible to bestir him to the necessary effort." Of a twenty-one-year-old girl, the doctor relates, "Her unfortunate father, who had hoped for so much from this operation, wrote that his daughter carefully shuts her eyes whenever she wishes to go about the house, especially when she comes to a staircase, and that she is never happier or more at ease than when, by closing her eyelids, she relapses into her former state of total blindness." A fifteen-year-old boy, who was also in love with a girl at the asylum for the blind, finally blurted out, "No, really, I can't stand it any more; I want to be sent back to the asylum again. If things aren't altered, I'll tear my eyes out."

Some do learn to see, especially the young ones. But it changes their lives. One doctor comments on "the rapid and complete loss of that striking and wonderful serenity which is characteristic only of those who have never yet seen." A blind man who learns to see is ashamed of his old habits. He dresses up, grooms himself, and tries to make a good impression. While he was blind he was indifferent to objects unless they were edible; now, "a sifting of values sets in . . . his thoughts and wishes are mightily stirred and some few of the patients are thereby led into dissimulation, envy, theft and fraud."

On the other hand, many newly sighted people speak well of the world, and teach us how dull is our own vision. To one patient, a human hand, unrecognized, is "something bright and then holes."

Shown a bunch of grapes, a boy calls out, "It is dark, blue and shiny. . . . It isn't smooth, it has bumps and hollows." A little girl visits a garden. "She is greatly astonished, and can scarcely be persuaded to answer, stands speechless in front of the tree, which she only names on taking hold of it, and then as 'the tree with the lights in it.'" Some delight in their sight and give themselves over to the visual world. Of a patient just after her bandages were removed, her doctor writes, "The first things to attract her attention were her own hands; she looked at them very closely, moved them repeatedly to and fro, bent and stretched the fingers, and seemed greatly astonished at the sight." One girl was eager to tell her blind friend that "men do not really look like trees at all," and astounded to discover that her every visitor had an utterly different face. Finally, a twenty-two-old girl was dazzled by the world's brightness and kept her eyes shut for two weeks. When at the end of that time she opened her eyes again, she did not recognize any objects, but, "the more she now directed her gaze upon everything about her, the more it could be seen how an expression of gratification and astonishment overspread her features; she repeatedly exclaimed: 'Oh God! How beautiful!'"

I saw color-patches for weeks after I read this wonderful book. It was summer; the peaches were ripe in the valley orchards. When I woke in the morning, color-patches wrapped round my eyes, intricately, leaving not one unfilled spot. All day long I walked among shifting color-patches that parted before me like the Red Sea and closed again in silence, transfigured, wherever I looked back. Some patches swelled and loomed, while others vanished utterly, and dark marks flitted at random over the whole dazzling sweep. But I couldn't sustain the illusion of flatness. I've been around for too long. Form is condemned to an eternal danse macabre with meaning: I couldn't unpeach the peaches. Nor can I remember ever having seen without understanding; the color-patches of infancy are lost. My brain then must have been smooth as any balloon. I'm told I reached for the moon; many babies do. But the color-patches of infancy swelled as meaning filled them; they arrayed themselves in solemn ranks down distance which unrolled and stretched before me like a plain. The moon rocketed away. I live now in a world of shadows that shape and distance color, a world where space makes a kind of terrible sense. . . .

When her doctor took her bandages off and led her into the garden, the girl who was no longer blind saw "the tree with the lights in it." It was for this tree I searched through the peach orchards of summer, in the forests of fall and down winter and spring for years. Then one day I was walking along Tinker Creek thinking of nothing at all and I saw the tree with the lights in it. I saw the backyard cedar where the mourning doves roost charged and transfigured, each cell buzzing with flame. I stood on the grass with the lights in it, grass that was wholly fire, utterly focused and utterly dreamed. It was less like seeing than like being for the first time seen, knocked breathless by a powerful glance. The flood of fire abated, but I'm still spending the power. Gradually the lights went out in the cedar, the colors died, the cells unflamed and disappeared. I was still ringing. I had been my whole life a bell, and never knew it until at that moment I was lifted and struck. I have since only very rarely seen the tree with the lights in it. The vision comes and goes, mostly goes, but I live for it, for the moment when the mountains open and a new light roars in spate through the crack, and the mountains slam.

Acknowledgments

Continued from page ii

The University of Georgia Press: "The Game," from *The Latin Deli: Prose & Poetry* by Judith Ortiz Cofer. Copyright © 1993 by Judith Ortiz Cofer. Reprinted by permission of The University of Georgia Press.

Arthur Cavanaugh: "Miss Awful" by Arthur Cavanaugh. Copyright © 1987 by Arthur Cavanaugh. Reprinted by permission of the author.

Peter Owen Ltd.: "A Man" by Nina Cassian, translated by Roy MacGregor-Hastie, from Bankier et al, *The Other Voice*, 1976. Reprinted by permission of Peter Owen Ltd., London.

HarperCollins Publishers, Inc.: Excerpt from "Seeing," from *Pilgrim at Tinker Creek* by Annie Dillard. Copyright © 1974 by Annie Dillard. Reprinted by permission of HarperCollins Publishers, Inc.